Are These Words Working For You?

▽

Find out by choosing the word that best completes each sentence.

1. Woody Allen is an excellent comedian because he has the ability to (*ad lib, importune*) on any occasion.
2. There is much concern over the decision to (*activate, ascertain*) the nuclear plant at Three Mile Island.
3. If you (*enterprise, minimize*) your overhead, your business will probably make a profit.
4. At one time, the term (*parody, scenario*) was used mainly when referring to film scripts. Now it is used for almost any hypothetical situation.
5. (*Pulchritude, Recalcitrance*) is one attribute that never goes out of favor.
6. When Henry Higgins complained of being (*bilious, restive*), he was referring to his liver, not his disposition.

➤   ➤

With *Super Vocabulary* you'll master thousands of valuable, topical words like these, *as they are used today, on subjects that are important to you*. So turn the page now... and start developing your dynamic, expanding vocabulary!

Answers: 1. ad lib, 2. activate, 3. minimize, 4. scenario, 5. pulchritude, 6. bilious

ALSO BY LEARN, INC.

Super Reading

Published by
WARNER BOOKS

SUPER VOCABULARY

LEARN, INC.

BY
Margaret Morgan Byrum

WARNER BOOKS

A Warner Communications Company

WARNER BOOKS EDITION

Warner Books, Inc.
666 Fifth Avenue
New York, N.Y. 10103

 A Warner Communications Company

Printed in the United States of America

First Printing: August, 1988

10 9 8 7 6 5 4 3 2 1

Welcome to a world of broader horizons, greater self-assurance, more favorable responses to your requests, and more pleasure in sharing your thoughts with others. Welcome to an expanded vocabulary.

Super Vocabulary was designed with you in mind. You've come this far in life with some ability to make your thoughts known to others through the use of words. You know that sometimes you can't find quite the word you need to communicate exactly what you mean. You want to enlarge your list of usable words—words you can call on when you need them to give precise thoughts, mental pictures, and shared dreams.

The benefits of an expanded and precise vocabulary are many:

- Clearer understanding of what you read
- Aid to logical and clear thinking
- Ability to better understand what you hear
- More color and precision in your writing and speaking
- Confidence that leads to success

It has long been recognized that the person who can express his or her thoughts clearly, precisely, and interestingly is the person who reaches the top, achieves goals, and enjoys the satisfaction of saying exactly what should be said in the least time possible.

You may have a usable vocabulary, but you want to add some fine tuning: create specific descriptions to replace generalities; develop varied ways to replace trite, overused expressions; include new words to add excitement to communication. We've tried to meet all these needs for you. We will discuss common words that are often misused or confused, less common words that can serve you in specific situations, words whose meanings vary in differing contexts, and some words that are just fun to know. Since the lists of "acceptable" words are constantly changing, we also include words that are emerging from specialized vocabularies to common use. When it is helpful to understand and use a word, we include some of its family history—its etymology.

Key words are used within the context of our discussion, not in isolation in a list. Instead of following an alphabetical sequence, words are grouped with words with which they share roots of origin, meanings, and specific needs, or with which they are confused.

Enjoy the program as you will the results! Learning anything new is not easy—you must want to expend the effort necessary to accomplish your goal. But we're certain you'll find the benefits are well worth the effort.

Bruce E. Corley

SUPER VOCABULARY

LEARN, INC.

SECTION I

SECTION 1

Introduction

You put your thoughts across with words. The words you use—and the ways you use them—will often be the reason why you do or don't get the results you want when you communicate with others.

Super Vocabulary offers not only groups of words and their meanings and uses, it gives you the tools for learning and for building a stronger and more varied vocabulary. The result is a confident *you*, in control of how others react to your words.

Let's elucidate that thought. The secret of expanding your usable vocabulary is, first, to be aware of unfamiliar words when you hear or read them. That means not just saying to yourself, "I don't know what that means," and then forgetting about it. Your goal is to develop a detective's interest in learning the meaning of any word you don't know.

That leads to the second secret: to have a good attitude about learning—to search for new and varied words that express your thoughts precisely.

Attitude is a vital ingredient. It helps to have a little Sherlock Holmes in you, to enjoy looking for clues that might lead to better understanding. Mentally answer any questions we ask you—just as you would in conversation. That gets you mentally involved.

Consider that word *elucidate*. Did you understand the word when it was used above? Were you aware of it? Did you try to guess the meaning in the context of the sentence?

Here's where we use one of Sherlock's tools: speculation. Take a guess on the meaning of the verb *elucidate*. If you speculated "make clear," or "explain," you're correct.

What we'd like you to do is guess or speculate on the meaning of any word you don't know. It doesn't matter if you're right or wrong. By speculating, you'll improve your recall and retention while building a powerful vocabulary.

Now, let's move to some of that speculating. Please read the directions and complete Pretest 1. (See p. 43 for the correct answers to the tests and exercises in this section.)

Pretest 1

Directions: Match the words in column A with the meanings in column B. On the line, write the word from column B that is *closest in meaning*.

A	B
1. elucidate _____	hint, suggest
2. nuance _____	shade of meaning
3. critique _____	mean
4. mnemonics _____	clarify
5. synonym _____	review carefully
6. denote _____	memory aids
7. connotation _____	deduce
8. imply _____	meaning the same
9. infer _____	suggested meaning

Section I, List 1

We're going to give you some tips on remembering and learning as we go along. For example, Groucho is a member of what family? Marx, of course. There are families of words, and if we associate words with their families, we can (1) remember them better, and (2) learn more words that are related.

Elucidate, for example, is from the same family as *lucid*, which means "clear." When you *elucidate*, you make things clear. Seeing the word *lucid* in print also helps you spell *elucidate*.

With one key word, you can expand your vocabulary by several words—if you know the family background. In fact, for some words you have to know something about the family to be able to understand all the nuances of the definitions.

Did you understand the word *nuance*? Let's look at that word before we return to the process we'd like you to follow throughout this book . . . and your entire life!

Nuance is a noun meaning a delicate degree or shade of difference. So looking at *nuances* of definitions means looking at fine, subtle variations in the definitions of words that mean almost the same thing.

> How about *critique* and *review*? Both mean an examination and an opinion—critiques or reviews of plays, projects, or proposals. But *critique* has the nuance of being more detailed and done by an expert. A *review* may be less detailed and may be submitted by any observer. The meanings from the root words—the grandfathers on the family word trees—are the combination of examining deliberately and looking again. Review doesn't have to be critical.

By the way, *critique* is frequently heard as a verb—to critique something. It is not yet accepted as a verb by language experts. Consider your audience before you speak about *critiquing* a political speech, for example. And— returning to the variation of meaning—if your boss says he has a *critique* of your report, you'll probably feel more apprehensive than if he says he has a *review* of it.

The *nuances* of words are very important, because words that mean almost the same thing can cause varying reactions in those to whom you wish to communicate your messages. We love buying bargains, great values, and clothes that are dramatically reduced in price. But we certainly don't want to wear *cheap* clothes. Advertising copywriters have long stressed *nuances*!

Let's talk about insurance.

We'd like you to be able to remember the words we review and add them to your permanent vocabulary. Here's how to do it. At the back of the book are pages containing lists of the words in the order in which we discuss them. For a vocabulary that continues to grow, cut out these lists and carry them and some blank 3 × 5-inch cards with you at all times. Use them in two ways:

> *First*, on the 3 × 5-inch cards, write the words you hear or read that you want to learn or clarify. If possible, write the sentence the word is in to remind yourself of the context in which the word is used. When you learn the meaning, write it down, then write a new sentence using that word. The result will be a personal dictionary of new words that you can file for your future reference.
>
> *Second*, use the lists and cards with time management skills. When you have a moment or two—possibly while sitting in a traffic jam, in a dentist's office, or waiting to see a client—take out your new words and study them. Just a few at a time will help you build the vocabulary you want.

Many people make a study of *mnemonics*, techniques in the art of remembering or aids that increase retention of information. Most memory courses use several of the techniques we've been discussing: observing, clarifying, writing, associating, and involving as many of your five senses as you can.

Studying a dictionary can, of course, help you to build an impressive vocabulary. However, few of us use dictionaries for that purpose. In addition, a dictionary meaning doesn't give you all the information you need to enlarge your usable vocabulary. It gives you precise meanings or *denotations* of words, root words, even basic grammar rules, and it offers synonyms—other words that have the same or similar meanings—but that isn't always enough to enable you to use the new words. A dictionary doesn't include *connotations*, *implications*, and *inferences*.

Let's look at the italicized words in the preceding paragraph. Have List 1 (cut out from the back of the book) before you as you continue reading. The word *denotation* is a noun signifying "meaning," especially a direct, specific meaning as distinct from an implied or related idea. Dictionaries *denote* clear, direct meanings. To *denote* may mean to serve as an indication of—as a frown *denotes* displeasure—but it does not require guessing. Something that is *denoted* is clear without interpretation.

The noun *connotation* means something that is suggested by a word or a thing, a suggested meaning in addition to the specific meaning. For example, "extreme poverty" *connotes* suffering—although the exact meaning, the *denotation*, does not specify that added association.

Imply and *infer* are another confusing pair. Do you know the difference? Mastery of sticky pairs like this one helps you to strengthen your vocabulary—if you can separate them.

> I'd *imply* my consent by my silence—my silence would *imply* my consent.

> Without really telling me so, you might *imply* that I don't stand a good chance of winning an election.

> You probably remember learning at an early age that rights *implied* obligations.

Imply means to suggest that something is so and refers to suggested meanings and possible consequences. The meaning of *infer* is very close to *imply* and is understandably confused with it. Use *infer* to mean to conclude from evidence or facts, to reason. Use *imply* to mean suggest or hint or refer to indirectly.

> You see smoke and *infer* that there's a fire.
> You observe a crowd gathered at an intersection and *infer* that there is an accident.
> You notice the parking lot at the ballpark is crowded and *infer* that there's a game.

Let's practice the nine words we've discussed so far before we go any further. The format is a repeating pattern for each group of words. First, take the *Pretest*, as you did on p. 5, for List 1, to see which words you already know, those you are uncertain about, and those that will be additions to your vocabulary.

The next step is a discussion of the words in the context of sentences, where we emphasize guidelines for remembering the words and how to use them. Having the list of words (cut out from the back of the book) in front of you adds reinforcement. The list numbers correspond to the pretest numbers.

The third step in the process is to practice using the words in application exercises. Writing the words helps you remember their spellings. And that's where we are now.

Read the directions carefully before you complete Exercise 1 and Exercise 2.

EXERCISE 1

Directions: Following each sentence is a set of four choices to fill the blank. On the line, write the word that is *closest in meaning* to the italicized word.

1. To *elucidate* a statement means to _____.
    defend it   deny it   explain it   argue with it

2. To understand the *nuances* of a language, one must be familiar with _____.
    roots   suffixes   overtones   literal meanings

3. When giving a *critique* of a play, the reviewer is concerned with _____ observation.
    superficial   detailed   disinterested   casual

4. *Mnemonics* concerns our _____ information.
    challenging   remembering   discussing
      cataloging

5. *Synonyms* are words that have _____ meanings
    different   opposite   similar   obvious

6. To *denote* usually means to _____ a word meaning.
    imply   indicate   speculate   organize

7. *Connotation* in language is a concern for the _____ a word has.
    sources   associations   pronunciations   spellings

8. To *imply* means to _____ that something is so.
    state   suggest   insist   demand

9. When we *infer* something, we usually mean that we reach our decisions by _____.
    chance   guess   evidence   hearsay

EXERCISE 2

Directions: Fill in each blank in the following paragraph with one of the following words:

> elucidate   critique   nuances   mnemonics
> synonym   denote   connotations
> imply   infer

In the morning paper there was a lengthy (1) _____ of the play that served to (2) _____ the difficult topic of physics. Although the title helped to (3) _____ the literal meaning of the play, the work was filled with many overtones and (4) _____. I don't mean to (5) _____ that it was a confusing work, but based on the evidence of the scenes, one could (6) _____ that it was a complicated drama. There were enough shades of meaning and (7) _____ to make me ponder the playwright's intent. I took some notes on the program. They'll serve as (8) _____ for future recall. I found the play confusing. If I had to produce another descriptive word for the play, creating a (9) _____ would be challenging.

If you are uncertain of the meaning or use of any of the words on Pretest 1, go back to the discussion of the meaning. Then follow through with the learning aids suggested earlier: listen to the way the word is used in conversation, look it up, note it on a card, *use* it. Review your memory aids until each word is a permanent part of your speaking and writing vocabulary.

Let's go on to the next group of words. They can all be used to describe what we'll try to do in this program. We'll restrict our effort to developing a *cognizance* of a few *germane* words for *succinct* messages and eliminate wandering to *extraneous cerebration*. Please complete Pretest 2 now.

Pretest 2

Directions: Match the words in column A with the meanings in column B. On the line, write the word from column B that is *closest in meaning*.

A		B
1. cognizance	_____	word beginning
2. germane	_____	unnecessary
3. succinct	_____	thinking
4. extraneous	_____	concise
5. cerebration	_____	pertinent, related
6. prefix	_____	understanding

Section I, List 2

The five key words used in the sentence above—*cognizance, germane, succinct, extraneous,* and *cerebration*—were all used in a discussion about communication. That's one way to remember them. Now let's look at each word.

You were going to develop *cognizance* of a few words. Within the context of that sentence, you might be able to guess that it means "understanding" or "knowing." If your ear is really tuned to word families, you might hear that *cognizance* is a member of the same family of a more familiar word, *recognize*.

There are several words that come from *cognoscere*, the Latin word meaning to "know."

Cognize is a verb meaning to "know" or to "understand."

Cognizant is an adjective meaning "knowledgeable" and "aware."

Cognizance is a noun meaning "knowledge" or "awareness."

So, to develop *cognizance* of a few *germane* words means you're building an awareness of a few *germane* words.

Germane, literally, means "having the same parents." It's used to mean "relevant" and "appropriate." "Closely related" and "pertinent" are other synonyms. We're concentrating on developing a list of words that are closely related to words we know, that can be used interchangeably with them.

Let's go back to the sentence. We mentioned *succinct* messages. From what family is that? The nouns *cinch*—notice that's c-i-n-c-h—and *cincture* both mean a "belt" or "sash" to tighten. They come from the same root word as *succinct*, which refers to a compressed, concise, and tightened message. That translates to no wasted words. Good business communication, for example, depends upon *succinct* writing. There's no place for an *extraneous* word or phrase when one well-chosen word will send the proper message.

Speaking of *extraneous*, our sentence referred to *extraneous cerebration*. You probably noticed the word *extra*, which means "more than is required or necessary." *Extraneous* is an adjective meaning "unnecessary" or "irrelevant." So an *extraneous* word is one that is not vital to conveying the intended message.

How about the final word in the cluster: *cerebration*? *Cerebration* is related to *cerebrum,* a part of the brain; *cerebral* is an adjective relating to the brain; *cerebration* is the act of *cerebrating,* of using the brain or thinking.

Extraneous cerebration, then, is unnecessary thinking. Can you use the adjective *cerebral* in a sentence?

> Playing chess is a *cerebral* activity—it requires mental involvement.

> A *cerebral* accident is a stroke, damage to an artery of the brain.

You may hear that last statement from your doctor. That's usually the way we learn the meaning of words—first, by listening to and imitating our parents; second, by listening to and imitating others. However, to build a more powerful vocabulary, you need to check the variations of meanings in differing contexts for *nuances.*

The last word on Pretest 2 was *prefix.* The meaning includes "coming before" or "beginning." To *prefix* a letter with an apology means to put the apology first. The *prefix* of a word is the beginning of it, a group of letters that helps you understand the meaning of the word because common prefixes have specific meanings.

After you complete Pretest 3, we'll look at some prefixes.

Please complete Exercise 3, Exercise 4, and Pretest 3 now.

EXERCISE 3

Directions: After each of the following words are four other words. Choose the one *closest in meaning* and write it on the line.

1. cognizant _____
   urbane   knowledgeable   unhappy   relevant

2. germane _____
   sickly   relevant   multiple   growing

3. extraneous _____
   essential   ordinary   foreign   unnecessary

4. succinct _____
   concise   overflowing   tasty   following

5. cerebration _____
   renewal   necessity   thinking   motivation

6. prefix _____
   root of word   beginning of word   end of word
   similar word

EXERCISE 4

Directions: Fill in each blank in the following paragraph with one of the following words:

cognizance   germane   succinct   extraneous
cerebration   prefix

Whereas a preface may begin a book, a (1) _____ will introduce a word. Recognition or (2) _____ of precise words enables us to select (3) _____ words relative to our thoughts and write brief, (4) _____ sentences without including unnecessary, (5) _____ ones that cause lengthy (6) _____ and mental anxiety in figuring out what response we expect.

Pretest 3

Directions: After each prefix listed below, write its meaning.

1. ab _____
2. ad _____
3. com or con _____
4. de _____
5. ex _____
6. in _____
7. in (another meaning) _____
8. pre _____
9. pro _____
10. re _____

Section I, List 3

One of the biggest challenges we face is time pressure: time to get the job done, time to learn ways to do things—even time to express our thoughts. How can we increase our vocabularies when we have so many time constraints?

If you're looking for a "quick fix," we have one to offer you. Called a *prefix,* it can help you attack new, unknown words for the rest of your life.

A prefix is the beginning of a word. What's the magic of a prefix? Since about 60 percent of our English words are of Latin origin, it makes sense to learn the meanings of the most common Latin prefixes. They offer keys to open the doors to so many meanings.

We'll work in alphabetical order. This should help you feel familiar with the prefixes rapidly, since you'll find you already know most of them. Let's start with the letter *a: ab* and *ad.*

Ab means "from" or "away."

> *Abnormal* is "away from normal."
>
> *Abstract* is "apart from application and association."

Ad means "to" or "toward."

> *Advance* means to "move toward" or to "move forward," to "progress."
>
> *Adhere* means to "stick to" (like glue) or to "follow" (*adhere* to the rules of a game).

Let's go to *c* and start with *com*, which means "with," "together," or "thoroughly."

> *Compress* means to "press together."
>
> *Combine* means to "bring together."
>
> *Compromise* literally means "making a promise together," or "mutually agreeing."

Sometimes the spelling is c-o-*n* instead of c-o-*m*, but it still means "together." The word *connote* means to "note with" or "associate."

There are six more words to learn right now, but before continuing, a reminder may be helpful. Remember that these prefixes aren't foolproof. English has many words from varied national backgrounds, so sometimes root words sound or look like Latin but come from another source. And sometimes the spelling of the prefix changes a bit because of the rest of the word. However, knowing the nine most common Latin prefixes is a running start for anyone who is serious about expanding vocabulary.

We've had *ab*, *ad*, and *com* or *con*.

Next is *de*. This prefix means "from," down," or "away."

> *Descend* means to "go down."
>
> *Decelerate* means to "slow down."
>
> *Deflect* means to "turn from" or "turn aside."
>
> *Denote*, the word we used earlier, means to "note from" or to "mean."

Next is *ex*, which means "out of," "from," or "former."

> *Excavate* means to "hollow out."
>
> *Exclude* means to "keep out."
>
> I know an *ex*-marine.

The prefix *in* means "in," "into," or "on."

> *Include* means to "take in," to "close in."
>
> *Increase* means to "grow in," as in size, amount, or number.

But how about *indefinite*? That means "not definite." *In*valid means "not valid." This is one of those cases where the word family shows its mixed ancestry. The prefix *in* can also mean "not." So, if you're looking for the meaning of a new word with *in* as a prefix, you may have to try both meanings: "in" or "not." Be cautious.

Our alphabetical list is growing. We have two *a*'s—*ab* and *ad;* one *c*—*com* or *con;* one *d*—*de;* one *e*—*ex;* and one *i*—*in*. All we have left are two *p*'s and an *r*. Then we'll start moving into the major vocabulary words for this lesson.

The first *p* is, naturally, *pre*. That means "before," "earlier than," "prior to." The word *prefix* is an example.

> *Preschool* means "before school."
>
> *Prefab* structures are made prior to shipping to the building site.
>
> *Predict* means to "declare in advance."
>
> *Prefer* means to "put before," as in ranking one thing above another.

The second *p* is *pro*. That means "forward" or "in favor of." *Prospect* doesn't sound like *pro*, but the spelling indicates that it is. It means to "look forward," as in to *prospect* for gold, or, "She's a good *prospect* for a job," a good possibility in the future.

> *Promote* means to "push forward" or to "move forward."

> *Propose* means to "put forward a plan or intention."

The last prefix to be introduced is *re*, which means "again" or "back."

> *React* means to "act against a stimulus."

> *Regain* means to "gain again."

> *Recognize* means to "know again." It doesn't have the sound we associate with *re*, but the spelling is there.

How about *reviewing* the prefixes—looking at them again? Then we'll move on to specific words.

You may find it helpful to break the nine prefixes into groups of three. It's easier to remember three short lists than one long one.

> The first alphabetical list is a-a-c: That's *ab*, *ad*, and *com* or *con*.

> Then there's d-e-i: *de*, *ex*, and *in*.

> And, finally, p-p-r: *pre*, *pro*, *re*.

For written practice in remembering and using prefixes, complete Exercise 5.

EXERCISE 5

Directions: After each prefix listed below, write its meaning and one word that uses it. (Some words have been discussed, and some are in the Answer Key (see p. 44). You may also use others.)

Prefix	Meaning	Word
1. ab–	_____	_____
2. ad–	_____	_____
3. com– or con–	_____	_____
4. de–	_____	_____
5. ex–	_____	_____
6. in–	_____	_____
7. in– (another)	_____	_____
8. pre–	_____	_____
9. pro–	_____	_____
10. re–	_____	_____

If you need to review any of the prefixes, go back and check their meanings and examples. When you feel confident, go on to Pretest 4, using prefixes in words.

Pretest 4

Directions: Match the words in column A with the meanings in column B. On the line, write the word from column B that is *closest in meaning*.

A	B
1. abdicate _____	scornful
2. abhor _____	patronizing
3. addendum _____	added to, attached
4. adjunct _____	detest
5. concomitant _____	profanity, meaningless expression
6. condescending _____	reconcile
7. delineate _____	addition
8. derisive _____	accompanying
9. ridiculous _____	draw, clarify
10. expiate _____	withdraw from
11. atone _____	make amends
12. expletive _____	absurd, laughable

Section I, List 4

Believing that repeated use is the best way to learn permanently, let's look at some words that use *prefixes*.

We'll begin with *abdicate,* using *ab.* How does the prefix help you know the meaning of the word?

"Well," you might reason, "it means to 'give' or to 'let go.' It could be stretched to mean to 'remove yourself' as when you're talking about abdicating a throne." Moving from what you already know to the next logical step prepares you for learning—and remembering.

Literally, *abdicate* means to "proclaim against." Usage includes to "cast off," to "discard," or to "renounce" a throne, a high office, a dignity, or a function. It's closely related to *resign* in meaning. However, *resign* implies giving up an unexpired office or trust, while *abdicate* implies evading a responsibility, as in *abdication* of the duties of a parent. Can you think of another *ab* word?

How about *abhor*? What association can you make to help you remember the meaning? You might remember that *ab* means "from," and *hor* could remind you of "horror." So, if something means "from" and reminds you of "horror," you don't like it.

> *Abhor* means to "loathe," "dislike intensely," "detest," "scorn," "turn from," "hate." You may *abhor* silence.

Let's look now at *addendum*. Because it uses the prefix *ad*, it must have the idea of "to" or "toward" in it somewhere. You might speculate that it's something added, an addition. And you'd be right.

> *Addendum* is often used to refer to a supplement to a book, but it can be another kind of addition.

> Do you ever think of an *addendum* you wish you'd added to your conversation?

Then there's the noun *adjunct*. It also means "added to" but not "a part of something else." It's used to mean an "associate" or "assistant," too.

The adjective *adjunct* has the same spelling and means "added" or "joined to" or "attached" in a subordinate or temporary capacity: an *adjunct* dentist, for example, joins an established one.

That brings us to the prefix *con* or *com*, and *concomitant*

has both. With both of those prefixes, you'd expect it to
mean "with."

It does—in a way. It combines the prefix *con* with a verb
meaning to "accompany." It means—you're right—"accompanying" or "being connected with." But the emphasis
is also one of time.

> *Coincident* applies to events occurring at the same
> time without implying a relationship.

> *Concomitant* refers to a *co*incidence in time of
> events that are so clearly related that one seems
> attendant on the other.

> *Accompaniment* is a synonym. You might observe
> that the loss of privacy is a *concomitant* to fame.
> They accompany each other consistently.

Consider how the meaning of *condescension* fits the
prefix.

> *Condescension* means voluntary descent from one's
> rank or dignity in relations with an inferior, a
> patronizing attitude or behavior. Literally it means
> to "descend with another"—that's where the pre-
> fix *con* comes in.

> The verb *condescend* means to "unbend," to
> "waive the privileges of rank." But it always
> includes a conscious attitude of superiority.

> If the company president *condescends* to eat in
> the cafeteria with the hourly employees, everyone
> is aware that he or she is consciously joining the
> lower level.

Next we have the prefix *de*. We have already discussed *denote* and *descend*.

Another word using the *de* prefix is *delineate*, literally meaning "from lines." We use it to mean "representing by drawn or painted lines" as in *delineating* ideas with a sketch to show them clearly. We also *delineate* narrow streets with strings of lights and *delineate* characters in books by supplying accurate details. Instructions can be the *delineation* of steps to build a tool shed. Sometimes *delineate* implies clear, accurate details instead of lines.

Also using the prefix *de* is *derisive*, the adjective, and *derision*, the noun. They refer to "laughing at." The word *ridiculous* has the same family root. They all have to do with laughter, as in scorn, not humor. Both *ridicule* and *deride* mean "to make the object of laughter."

> *Ridicule* implies deliberate and often malicious belittling, as, "He consistently *ridiculed* everything she said."

> *Deride* suggests bitter ridicule, as, "She *derided* their attempt to improve their vocabulary."

When you offend people by *deriding* their efforts, you may have to seek *expiation* before you'll be forgiven. Doing favors for them might be the means of *atonement*, of making amends, to extinguish the guilt.

The verb *expiate* means to "atone for," to "appease." So, seeking *expiation* means seeking a peaceful at-one-ment and removal of offense, a reconciliation.

Another removal is often mentioned with the noun *expletive* as in "expletive deleted." Interestingly, that phrase is a recent popular use of *expletive;* it gained popularity with the transcription of the Watergate tapes.

The first meaning of *expletive* is "serving to fill a vacancy without adding meaning." *Oh* is a common *expletive*. It adds no meaning to a sentence.

The second definition of *expletive* is a "meaningless expression of profanity." Basically, of course, profanity adds no meaning—just emotion. We may describe someone's limited command over words as a "collection of expletives," meaning "words with little meaning."

Let's do a quick review of the words using prefixes. Words using *ab* and *ad:*

Abdicate means to "renounce," and *abhor* means to "hate."

Addendum and *adjunct* both mean "added parts," additions, with *adjunct* often meaning "assistant."

Words using *com* or *con:*

Concomitant means "accompanying," and *condescension* means "consciously lowering rank."

Words using *de:*

Delineate means "using lines or clear details to make clear."

Deride means to "ridicule bitterly." *Ridicule* means "to make the object of laughter," often maliciously.

Words using *ex:*

Expiate means to "atone for a past offense," and *expletives* are filler words with no meaning.

Now complete Exercises 6 and 7 to make that cluster of words yours. Then complete Pretest 5.

EXERCISE 6

Directions: On the lines in the following sentences, write the words in parentheses that *best fit the meanings* of the sentences.

1. The king was in no mood to _____ (*abdicate, expiate*), even though his subjects had hoped to be rid of him.

2. If young people would _____ (*delineate, abhor*) horror movies, Hollywood would not make so many of them.

3. An already overly long book review does not need a lengthy _____ (*addendum, expletive*).

4. The fact that he was _____ (an *adjunct,* a *concomitant*) professor rather than a permanent member of the faculty did not affect his teaching ability.

5. The _____ (*atonement, concomitant*) nature of the baseball, basketball, and hockey seasons makes it difficult to follow a favorite team.

6. If a parent treats his children with continual _____ (*addendum, condescension*), he will lose their respect.

7. An outstanding sports announcer can _____ (*expiate, delineate*) the plays on a video screen with little trouble.

8. When George Orwell was asked in India to shoot an enraged elephant, he was most concerned with the _____ (*derisive, expletive*) scorn of the crowd.

9. If a novelty song contains no meaning, musicians soon see it as _____ (an *abhorrent,* a *ridiculous*) ditty.

10. In olden times, to _____ (*delineate, expiate*) their guilt, people went around in sackcloth.

11. The husband who forgot to take out the trash sought _____ (*atonement, addendum*) from his wife with a shortcake from the bakery.

12. There is a modern concern that rock lyrics have an _____ (*expletive, expiation*) in every stanza.

EXERCISE 7

Directions: Fill in each blank in the next six sentences with one of the following words:

abdication　　abhorrence　　addendum　　adjunct
concomitant　　condescension

1. _____ is an adjective meaning a "consistent accompaniment" or "coinciding in time."

2. _____ means "intense dislike," "hate."

3. _____ is a noun meaning an "added part," a "supplement."

4. _____ is an adjective meaning "added" or "joined to," "attached."

5. _____ means to "renounce responsibilities or duties."

6. _____ means a descent from rank, an unbending, patronization.

Directions: Fill in the next five blanks with one of these words:

atone   delineate   derision   expiate   expletive

7. Two words that mean to "appease" or to "reconcile" are _____ and _____.

8. Another word for *ridicule* is _____.

9. An often profane word with little meaning is an _____.

10. To give a clear picture through lines or details is to _____.

Pretest 5

Directions: Match the words in column A with the meanings in column B. On the line, write the word from column B that is *closest in meaning*.

A		B
1. induce	_____	dubious
2. inadvertently	_____	enormous
3. precept	_____	unintentionally
4. prodigious	_____	renewal
5. propinquity	_____	lead to
6. resurgence	_____	principle, example
7. anomalous	_____	nearness
8. apocryphal	_____	ominous
9. portentous	_____	irregular

Section I, List 5

Let's share a few words that use the remaining prefixes.

These are *in*, *pre*, *pro*, and *re*. I might try to *induce* you to *inadvertently* include a comment on the *precept* you established with your *prodigious* ability to respond to my suggestions.

You see the word *induce*. That means to "lead on," to "cause," to "provide *inducement* or motive for action." And *inadvertently* means "not meaning to," "unintentionally." So I'm trying to get you to unintentionally mention what a good *precept* you set, what a good example you are, with your *prodigious* ability, your enormous ability, to react to my suggestions.

We made several points there! *Induce* means to "lead to," and *inadvertently* means "not meaning to."

> You may ask, "Is there an *advertent* without the prefix *in*"? Yes, there is, and it means just what you think it should: "heedful" or "giving attention to."

> *Inadvertent* uses the prefix *in* to mean "not giving attention to."

To establish a *precept*—literally to "instruct beforehand" —is to set up a command or a principle to be used as a rule for future action, to be an example of what should be done. Its root means to "drive forward," to "be ahead of."

Propinquity uses the prefix *pro*. It means "near to," in place, time, or even in blood—as the *propinquity* of a "kissin' cousin."

For the last prefix, *re*, we'll use *resurgence*, meaning to "surge again." In context, it often comes to mean "being reborn," "rising again to life."

> At the present time, we have a *resurgence* of interest in things Victorian.

This is a good time to remind you that the vocabulary you're building will be equally useful in speaking and in writing. Let's look at some words that describe writing. Writing can be *anomalous*, *apocryphal*, or *portentous*.

An *anomalous* report is one that is inconsistent with the normal, not what's expected or usual. Your business reports are all *germane* and *succinct*, of course.

> An example of an *anomaly*, the noun form of *anomalous*, is writing the minutes of a business meeting, say, in poetry form. It would be unusual, irregular.

Now let's examine the word *apocryphal*. You may have heard of the Apocrypha but not be sure what it is. The Apocrypha is a group of early religious writings, many of which are not accepted by Jews or Christians because of doubt about historic authenticity. It follows that *apocryphal* writing is writing of doubtful authenticity.

> *Fictitious* is often used as a synonym for *apocryphal*, but nuance makes it a poor substitute. *Fictitious* means made up, invented, or imagined; *apocryphal* means of questionable authenticity or from a dubious source. There's a difference between a *fictitious* statement and an *apocryphal* one.

Any idea what *portentous* writing is, writing that is a *portent*?

The verb *portend* means to "anticipate," often to "give warning."

The noun *portent* is from the same Latin root and is an omen, something that foreshadows a coming event—usually an unpleasant event.

The adjective *portentous* usually means "ominous." A *portentous* announcement is a weighty warning of something that will follow.

When a company is in financial difficulty, an invitation of all personnel to a meeting is *portentous*.

Let's review those three words. *Anomalous* means "unexpected and unusual," *apocryphal* means "of questionable validity," and *portentous* means "ominous, forewarning."

It's now time to get a picture of your progress. Please complete Exercises 8 and 9. After taking Pretest 6, we'll continue with List 6.

EXERCISE 8

Directions: Fill in each blank in the following sentences with the word that *best fits the meaning* of the sentence.

1. Mrs. Fox could not _____ her children to eat green vegetables.

     seduce   induce   adduce   perceive

2. The golfer _____ hit his opponent's ball by mistake.

    inadvertently   forcefully   purposefully
       irregularly

3. One _____ that Ben Franklin seemed to follow was "A penny saved is a penny earned."

    misanthrope   portent   precept   prefix

4. The _____ amount of wheat grown on the farms became more of a bane than a boon when the market price dropped.

    meager   ominous   portentous   prodigious

5. The ladies of the bridge club shared a _____ that went beyond their meeting each Thursday afternoon.

    alienation   menu   propinquity   omen

6. The _____ of Japan as a leading economic power is one of the marvels of modern times.

    precepts   apocryphal   resurgence   addendum

7. Just when you think you have your income tax form filled in correctly, there is some _____ section that throws you off balance.

    derisive   atonement   anomalous   expletive

8. Modern biographies seem interested in dramatic action that is _____ rather than based on historical facts.

    inadvertent   apocryphal   tentative
       portentous

9. The first news of President Reagan's being shot was a _____ announcement.

    inadvertent   resurgent   portentous
       concomitant

EXERCISE 9

Directions: Fill in each blank in the following paragraph with one of the following words.

anomalous	induce	prodigious
apocryphal	portentous	propinquity
inadvertent	precept	resurgence

The American government is trying to (1) _____ the general public to save more money. It could be (2) _____, that the government is spending more than ever as though a main (3) _____ were (4) _____ spending. If the government says to save on one hand while spending on the other, we are faced with an (5) _____ situation that will lead to a (6) _____ of higher interest rates. Adding to this (7) _____ situation is the excessive amount of imports while exports decline. The (8) _____ of friendly neighbors to our north and south has not alleviated the trade imbalance. Many pretend this economic condition is (9) _____, but it is based on facts and figures.

Pretest 6

Directions: Match the words in column A with the meanings in column B. On the line, write the word from column B that is *closest in meaning*.

A	B
1. erudite _____	bitter, harsh
2. esoteric _____	argumentative, belligerent
3. enigma _____	praise
4. cacophony _____	puzzle
5. dissonance _____	perfect example, model
6. corroboration _____	hidden, secret
7. homogeneity _____	displaying great knowledge
8. acrimonious _____	flagrantly wicked
9. bellicose _____	disharmony, harsh-sounding
10. nefarious _____	confirmation, support
11. accolade _____	noise, lack of agreement
12. paragon _____	imitate
13. emulate _____	similarity, uniformity

Section I, List 6

Communication may be *erudite, esoteric,* or a complete *enigma.*

All begin with the letter *e* and all can be used to describe communication. Therefore, they must all be adjectives.

The first, *erudite*, means "displaying great knowledge."

A person who is *erudite* is well read and scholarly, displaying impressive learning and *erudition*—the noun form that especially refers to knowledge acquired from books. The person might be called learned, and would surely present his information *eruditely*—the adverb form.

Esoteric means "hidden" or "secret," designed for and understood by the specially initiated. Since it is limited to a small circle, it also has come to mean "confidential" or "private."

Esoteric meanings are revealed to only a select few.

When information is coded for a small group, the true meaning may remain an *enigma*. *Enigma* is a noun meaning a "puzzle," a "mystery," or a "riddle."

Although *mystery* is considered a synonym of *enigma*, anything that is hard to understand or explain is considered *enigmatic*, the adjective form. *Enigmatic* writing is purposely obscure.

Are *enigmas* always *esoteric*? No, but it's a good question to ask.

An *enigmatic* report is hard to understand because the meaning is difficult or not explained clearly.

An *esoteric* report is difficult to understand because it was intended for a select group of readers.

Let's look at two words that describe sound and are usually associated with music: *cacophony* and *dissonance*.

Cacophony is a noun meaning "noise," "disharmony," "discordant sounds." Its emphasis is on the harshness in the sound—whether in music or in words—so it really means "harsh-sounding."

> In your business communication you might refer to the *cacophony* of a meeting when everyone was talking at once.

Since *dissonance* is a noun with a similar meaning—noise, discord, disharmony—the emphasis on lack of agreement can be applied to many business settings.

> When a negotiation meeting that was called to establish cooperation between two groups becomes an accusing session, discord and *dissonance* result. *Dissonance* is best used in the nonmusical sense when it applies to an inconsistency between beliefs and actions.

To summarize, both *cacophony* and *dissonance* mean "unpleasant noise," with *dissonance* having the possibility of inconsistency between beliefs and actions.

Now let's look at some words used to denote agreement. *Corroboration* and *homogeneity* indicate good working conditions. To *corroborate* means to "confirm," to "support with evidence or authority," to "make certain." So, *corroboration* is confirmation, support—may even be proof.

> When you announce a startlingly new theory to your *erudite* colleagues, you must make them *cognizant* of all your *corroborating* evidence.

That was a good sentence for reviewing some of the words we talked about earlier. Now let's get back to the word *homogeneity*. You know the related verb, *homogenize:* you probably buy *homogenized* milk. To *homogenize* milk is to break up the fat globules into very fine particles of uniform size and evenly distribute them.

> *Homogeneity* means "having identical distribution of functions or values," as in the *homogeneity* of two statistical surveys.

Before we become too friendly, let's consider some sour or uncomplimentary words. They're useful in dealing with people who are *acrimonious*, *bellicose*, and *nefarious*.

Those are all adjectives that depict people in less than the best possible light. *Acrimonious* means "bitter," "harsh," or "caustic," especially in feeling, language, and manner. You may know the related adjective *acrid*, which describes a harsh taste or pungent odor.

> When you have an *acrimonious* dispute, you may find it leaves an *acrid* taste in your mouth.

> *Acrimonious* neighbors do not help *homogeneity* in a neighborhood.

> *Acrimony* may eat at any good relationship—like acid.

Acrimony might even make you *bellicose*—argumentative, belligerent, inclined to start quarrels or wars. Synonyms for *bellicose* are "warlike," "quarrelsome," "pugnacious."

> We suspect that *bellicose* people would rather fight than switch!

The last word we're discussing now is *nefarious*, as in *nefarious* schemes—a scheme that is flagrantly wicked, evil, or possibly impious. The Latin root means "not according to divine law." A synonym is "vicious."

> Neighbors with *nefarious* schemes don't add to *homogeneity*, either.

> You read about a lot of *nefarious* schemes in the history of England.

We can end this group of words on a more pleasant note. Let's talk about people we like and admire. Let's give out some *accolades*, attempt to *emulate* them, and consider them *paragons*.

The word *accolade* really began with the ceremony of conferring knighthood. Literally it's "a blow on the shoulder with the flat of a sword." But we use it to indicate praise, honor, or an award that is bestowed as a mark of acknowledgment or superiority.

To *emulate* means to "imitate." In fact, it can even mean to "strive to excel"—not only to be as good as, but to be better than. That keeps *paragons* on their toes!

A *paragon* is a perfect example and model, a goal for others to work toward. That's not a bad word to end this group of vocabulary builders!

> **Reminder:** Become aware of new words you read and hear. Develop the habit of writing them down, preferably in the context of a sentence. Use a dictionary to nail down precise meanings and discover family trees and mnemonics, and write those with each new word. Then use the word...use the lists to review...and use the word some more.

Work the system, and you'll make this vocabulary system work for you.

Please complete Exercises 10 and 11 now. If, after completing all the exercises, you still feel unsure of some of the words—unable either to recognize them in context or to use them correctly—begin again with Exercise 1 for a review; that will result in greater assurance in using your expanded vocabulary.

EXERCISE 10

Directions: On the lines in the following paragraph, write the words in parentheses that *best fit the meanings* of the sentences.

The (1) _____ (*erudite, nefarious*) adult schoolteacher was always looking for (2) _____ (*acrimonious, esoteric*) meanings, even in short stories of a straightforward nature without a trace of an (3) _____ (*enigma, accolade*). Of course, in the classroom with a (4) _____ (*cacophony, corroboration*) of sounds, discussion was difficult. This led to conflicting opinions and a (5) _____ (*dissonance, homogeneity*) of views. There was little (6) _____ (*dissonance, homogeneity*) of opinions, little similarity of viewpoints. Fortunately, there was one outstanding student who served as (7) _____ (a *paragon*, an *accolade*) for the others. When discussions became nasty and (8) _____ (*acrimonious, nefarious*), he would quiet the most (9) _____ (*esoteric, bellicose*) students who wanted to fight over the issue. If there was any (10) _____ (*nefarious, esoteric*) plan to disrupt conversation, this student could also (11) _____ (*emulate, erudite*) the teacher and offer (12) _____ (*enigmas,*

accolades) to the least boisterous. He excelled in offering
(13) _____ (*dissonance, corroboration*) of any sound
idea proposed.

EXERCISE 11

Directions: Fill in each blank in the following sentences
with the word that *best fits the meaning* of the sentence.

1. The librarian was accustomed to dealing with many
   learned and _____ professors whose language
   was hard to understand.
   paragon   bellicose   erudite   vapid

2. If checkers is a rather easy game, chess should be
   called _____.
   diffident   homogeneous   esoteric   provincial

3. Sherlock Holmes could solve almost any _____,
   much to Watson's amazement.
   enigma   editorial   condescension   romance

4. A _____ of sounds came from the school cafe-
   teria daily.
   delineation   paragon   cacophony   jargon

5. Members of the debating team thought they had agreed
   on a topic, but they suddenly found themselves with a
   genuine case of _____.
   complacency   dissonance   resonance
   articulation

6. Without the _____ of the Senate, the president has difficulty passing his choice of legislation.
   abdication   rudeness   disparagement
   corroboration

7. The problem with too much _____ in any organization is a feeling of dullness.
   laxity   homogeneity   corroboration
   perplexity

8. The guest speaker was shocked at the _____ nature of the questions from the audience.
   plaintive   acrimonious   mnemonic
   persuasive

9. The situation in northern Ireland has long been in a _____ state.
   pleasant   bellicose   virtuous   ethical

10. Some say the shooting of the pope was a _____ scheme with roots in Bulgaria.
    nefarious   negligent   inoffensive   pacifying

11. Winners at the Olympics receive many _____ beyond the awarding of medals.
    dispatches   coronets   emulations   accolades

12. It is often difficult for a child to _____ actions of an outstanding parent.
    emulate   expiate   abdicate   connote

13. Few would doubt that Mother Theresa is a _____ of virtue.
    enigma   mnemonic   paragon   cacophony

ANSWER KEY—SECTION I

Pretest 1

1. clarify
2. shade of meaning
3. review carefully
4. memory aids
5. meaning the same
6. mean
7. suggested meaning
8. hint, suggest
9. deduce

Exercise 1

1. explain it
2. overtones
3. detailed
4. remembering
5. similar
6. indicate
7. associations
8. suggest
9. evidence

Exercise 2

1. critique
2. elucidate
3. denote
4. connotations
5. imply
6. infer
7. nuances
8. mnemonics
9. synonym

Pretest 2

1. understanding
2. pertinent, related
3. concise
4. unnecessary
5. thinking
6. word beginning

Exercise 3

1. knowledgeable
2. relevant
3. unnecessary
4. concise
5. thinking
6. beginning of word

Exercise 4

1. prefix
2. cognizance
3. germane
4. succinct
5. extraneous
6. cerebration

Pretest 3

1. from, away
2. to, toward
3. with, together, thoroughly
4. from, down, away
5. out of, from, former
6. in, into, on
7. not
8. before, earlier than, prior to
9. forward, in favor of
10. again, back

Exercise 5
(some possible answers)

1. abstract, abstain
2. adhere, adjunct
3. combine, commune
4. denote, defend
5. ex-marine, ex-patriot
6. inhale, induce
7. inactive, incomplete
8. prefab, preschool
9. promote, produce
10. regain, recognize

Pretest 4

1. withdraw from
2. detest
3. addition
4. added to, attached
5. accompanying
6. patronizing
7. draw, clarify
8. scornful
9. absurd, laughable
10. make amends
11. reconcile
12. profanity, meaningless expression

Exercise 6

1. abdicate
2. abhor
3. addendum
4. an adjunct
5. concomitant
6. condescension
7. delineate
8. derisive
9. a ridiculous
10. expiate
11. atonement
12. expletive

Exercise 7

1. concomitant
2. abhorrence
3. addendum
4. adjunct
5. abdicate
6. condescension
7. atone, expiate
8. derision
9. expletive
10. delineate

Pretest 5

1. lead to
2. unintentionally
3. principle, example
4. enormous
5. nearness
6. renewal
7. irregular
8. dubious
9. ominous

Exercise 8

1. induce
2. inadvertently
3. precept
4. prodigious
5. propinquity
6. resurgence
7. anomalous
8. apocryphal
9. portentous

Exercise 9

1. induce
2. inadvertent
3. precept
4. prodigious
5. anomalous
6. resurgence
7. portentous
8. propinquity
9. apocryphal

Pretest 6

1. displaying great knowledge
2. hidden, secret
3. puzzle
4. disharmony, harsh-sounding
5. noise, lack of agreement
6. confirmation, support
7. similarity, uniformity
8. bitter, harsh
9. argumentative, belligerent
10. flagrantly wicked
11. praise
12. perfect example, model
13. imitate

Exercise 10

1. erudite
2. esoteric
3. enigma
4. cacophony
5. dissonance
6. homogeneity
7. a paragon
8. acrimonious
9. bellicose
10. nefarious
11. emulate
12. accolades
13. corroboration

Exercise 11

1. erudite
2. esoteric
3. enigma
4. cacophony
5. dissonance
6. corroboration
7. homogeneity
8. acrimonious
9. bellicose
10. nefarious
11. accolades
12. emulate
13. paragon

SECTION II

Did you learn the words in the first section? Do you feel comfortable with them? Are they really becoming a part of your usable vocabulary?

You may recognize many of them and know their meanings when you see them but still not know them well enough to use them in conversation. That's understandable; you've seen these words for years and not used them. Mastery won't come overnight, but you can enjoy your progress as you keep applying the system.

It's worth the effort to find time to write what you want to learn. That's why we ask you to write the words in the exercises instead of just matching numbers and letters. You don't need practice in writing letters; you need practice in writing new words and their meanings. There are other mnemonics—other memory/learning aids—but few compete with writing in overall effectiveness. The words are, of course, printed for you, too. Try testing yourself with the printed lists (which appear at the back of the book) as soon as you can after finishing each set of words.

When buying a dictionary, make sure that it was published recently. Many of those "brand new," shiny dictionaries that appear in bookstores were published eight to ten years ago, so they do not have the latest words. Looking at the publication date is a standard skill in surveying possible resources—and that bit of information is *serendipity*.

Serendipity means the "aptitude to find valuable or agreeable things unexpectedly, without looking for them." Following is some *serendipitous* guidance before you buy any nonfiction book—dictionaries included. Learn as much as you can from what's on the cover and in the early pages of the book. It's like looking for an animal's *pedigree*—an ancestral line, the purity of the breed, any distinguished ancestry. So, read about the authors and their track record, about the research done for reference books, the number of times the book has been printed, and the latest copyright and publication dates.

Effective learning is not a passive activity. You have to become involved mentally, not remain a spectator. Here's one more learning aid before we continue: pronounce words aloud. That, too, is involvement and adds another of the senses to reinforce learning.

In this section, we'll discuss another fifty words, some of which use the prefixes we learned in Section I. A few more prefixes, some common suffixes, and some common word families are also presented. The first step is to complete Pretest 1 for Section II. (See p. 92 for the correct answers to the tests and exercises in this section.)

Pretest 1

Directions: Match the words in column A with the meanings in column B. On the line, write the word from
column B that is *closest in meaning*.

A	B
1. serendipity _____	turning point
2. pedigree _____	unexpected occurrence needing action
3. exigency _____	ancestral line
4. emergency _____	desperate
5. contingency _____	aptitude for making fortunate discoveries
6. crisis _____	tight place, narrow passage
7. dire _____	urgency
8. strait _____	untangle, free
9. extricate _____	possibility

Section II, List 1

Let's begin with some words that cause confusion. Some
are fairly common. For example, what's the difference
between *exigency* and *emergency*?

Exigency is a noun that means "urgency" or a "situation
calling for immediate action." A third meaning includes
"pressing needs" or "demands."

> In talking of people, the adjective *exigent* means
> "very demanding": if the sales manager is *exigent*,
> she may be reflecting the demands made upon
> her.

Referring to situations, *exigent* means "urgent," "requiring action."

The noun *exigency* means either "pressure urgently applied" or a "situation requiring action."

The *exigency* of the moment requires drastic action. The *exigency* of a time schedule demands immediate decisions.

Emergency is sometimes given as a synonym. However, here we get into nuances again. An *emergency* is generally an unexpected occurrence or set of circumstances that needs attention. A flood may create an *emergency,* a situation needing immediate action.

Exigency may refer to such a situation or to the need arising from it, but it stresses the pressure of restrictions or the urgency of the demand created by the situation.

The same unforeseen flood may create an *emergency* to be watched, but when a town is endangered, the *exigency* demands action.

Along the same line, where do *contingency* and *crisis* fit? You may hear these words from an engineer friend in connection with nuclear power, for example.

The noun *contingency* refers to an event—as an emergency— that is possible but not certain. In testing nuclear plants, they plan for every *contingency*—every possibility.

Crisis refers to an event regarded as a turning point, the crucial point at which success or failure is known—like the *crisis* of a disease when the fever finally breaks.

In planning the test, the power company considered every *contingency* and sighed with relief
when the smooth functioning indicated they'd
passed the *crisis* and no unexpected *emergency* or
exigency demanded action.

Your engineer friend will be glad the situation didn't leave
him in *dire straits*. Those words mean a messy situation—
usually one from which it's difficult to extricate oneself.

Dire means "desperate," "extreme," or "oppressive."
A sudden loss of power would leave the power company in
dire straits, in an extremely serious situation.

Did you notice the word *extricate*? It means to "untangle,"
to "free from a difficult position." It implies the use of
great care—more care than just to free something. The
adjective *strait* means "closely fitting," "tight," "constricted."
You've heard of a *strait*jacket.

Have you noticed how grouping words relating to one
situation or those having slightly different meanings makes
learning less painful—acts as an *anesthetic*. Or is it *anesthesia*?

That's a good pair to discuss, but first let's review the
nine words we've just examined. Please complete Exercises
1 and 2 and Pretest 2. Then we'll attack that *anesthetic*
problem.

EXERCISE 1

Directions: On the following lines, write the words that are
closest in meaning.

1. serendipity _____
    nervous disorder   ability to find the unexpected
      sad music   claustrophobia

2. pedigree _____
    ancestral line   hair style   learning experience
      foot doctor

3. exigency _____
    delay   planned action   stalling tactic
      urgency

4. emergency _____
    stable condition   unexpected occurrence
      new growth   hemorrhage

5. contingency _____
    landmark   direct route   possible option
      containment

6. crisis _____
    unexpected emergency   stable   placid mood
      turning point

7. dire _____
    desire   desperate   aflame   placid

8. strait _____
    tight place, narrow passage   proper   ethics
      accurate drawing

9. extricate _____
    resign   motivate   untangle   snarl

EXERCISE 2

Directions: On the lines in the following sentences, write the words in parentheses that *best fit the meanings* of the sentences.

1. When looking for my golf clubs, I found a long-lost tennis racket. I hoped this pleasant surprise might indicate that I had _____ (*contingency, serendipity*) and never realized it.
2. Horse breeders are often more concerned about the _____ (*strait, pedigree*) of a horse than about its outward appearance.
3. When John broke his leg, he was taken directly to the _____ (*emergency, contingency*) room at the hospital.
4. If all the doors are locked, the administrator has _____ (a *contingency*, an *exigency*) plan for entering the building.
5. Once the boy began telling lies to his mother, he found it difficult to _____ (*implicate, extricate*) himself from the unpleasant situation.
6. In a time of _____ (*serendipity, crisis*) a calm voice is welcomed.
7. When you go to the bank and find that you've overdrawn your account, the situation is _____ (*dire, extricating*).
8. Even the experienced pilot had difficulty going through the _____ (*straits, straights*) of Panama.
9. The president told the Senate of the _____ (*contingency, exigency*) concerning the tax bill; legislation had to be passed before the chamber recessed.

Pretest 2

Directions: Match the meanings in column A with the
words in column B. On the line, write the word from
column B that is *closest in meaning*.

A	B

A   **B**

1. condition, rank _____ anesthetic
2. standard for judgment _____ anesthesiology
3. gas or drug used to produce loss of
   feeling _____ anesthetist
4. one branched candlestick _____ anesthesiologist
5. a doctor who specializes in
   anesthesia _____ data
6. one layer _____ status
7. fact or facts, information _____ stratum
8. observable event _____ candelabra
9. technician trained to administer
   anesthetic _____ agenda
10. science of loss of feeling _____ criterion
11. planned schedule _____ phenomenon

Section II, List 2

Anesthetic and *anesthesia* aren't unfamiliar words, but they
certainly do cause confusion—and consequently, uncertainty. Do you know the difference between an *anesthetist* and
an *anesthesiologist*? Let's establish some associations, some
mnemonics.

> An *anesthesiologist* is someone who has medical
> training, who is an M.D. before specializing in
> *anesthetics*. An *anesthesiologist* specializes in the
> science of *anesthesia;* that is, a partial or total

loss of the sense of feeling. The suffix, *ologist*, indicates one who is an authority after study. Group it with biologist and geologist, experts in other fields.

Anesthesia may be induced by an *anesthetic*, a drug or gas used to produce *anesthesia*.

An *anesthetist* is a nurse or technician trained to administer *anesthetics*.

They aren't so confusing when you explain them that way, are they?

Now let's look at some common mispronunciations. They can be as embarrassing as using the wrong word. A couple that are very common are *data* and *status*.

For those who took Latin—and that number is diminishing rapidly—the correct pronunciation is well established and the mispronunciations are irritating. But these are words in the midst of change. The short *a* pronunciations aren't the preferred pronunciation yet, but they're coming down the homestretch. Listening to radio or television would lead you to believe they'd made it already. To reinforce both the value of a recently published dictionary and the changes taking place, let's look at three dictionaries.

In *Webster's Handy College Dictionary*, published in 1976, *dāta* with a long *a* was the only pronunciation given. By 1981, *dăta*, with the *a* sounding like the *a* in "ash," was given as a second possibility.

In *Webster's Ninth New Collegiate Dictionary*, published in 1983, there were three possibilities: *dāta*, *dăta*, and *däta*.

That is a good illustration of the fact that dictionaries follow usage and do not set it. To avoid the "anything goes" conclusion, let's say that if enough people say it often enough, it becomes acceptable. The same is true of *stātus*, the other word mentioned, and *strāta*. Although the long *a*'s are still first pronunciations, short ones are now mentioned.

What about plurals? Do dictionaries stick to the Latin endings of *um* for singular and *a* for plural: *datum* and *data*, *stratum* and *strata*?

> Webster's notes that, although it is still occasionally marked with disapproval, *data* is well established both as a singular and as a plural noun and is regularly used as a mass noun denoting a collection of material. In that sense, *data* means "information" or a "collection of facts."

Data processing means plural pieces of information rather than singular, but you never hear of *datum* processing when there's only one fact entered into a computer. However, the singular—*datum*—is still correct when it means the "basis for reasoning or calculating or measuring." In that case, the acceptable plural is *datums*, but that use and meaning isn't as common as *data*, meaning "information."

Strata, along with *criteria* and *phenomena*, may eventually become established and acceptable for both singular and plural, but now one layer is a *stratum*, and more than one are *strata*.

How about *criteria* and *phenomena*? *Criterion*, singular, means a "characterizing mark or trait," a "standard for basing judgment or evaluation." However, it is usually used in the plural, as in the *criteria* for evaluating classic cars or prize-winning dogs.

A *phenomenon* is an observable fact or event, something that happens. We often use the adjective form, *phenomenal,* to mean "extraordinary" or "remarkable"—a *phenomenal* success or a *phenomenal* bore.

Do remember that, although *criteria* and *phenomena* may someday be completely acceptable as singular nouns, at the present time the singulars are *criterion* and *phenomenon*.

There are two more. *Candelabra* is what we call one branched candlestick or lamp, and we add an *s* for more than one. *Agenda* is the same. We use *agendas* for the planned schedules for more than one meeting. These formerly plural endings with *a* are now accepted as singular.

Let's review the twenty words we've discussed so far.

We began with a discussion of dictionaries, then let you use some *serendipity* about surveying a book before handing over the cash.

> *Serendipity* is the act of discovering an unexpected, unasked for, but agreeable bonus. Surveying, we said, is like tracing the *pedigree* of the dog you're considering buying.

> *Pedigree* is the ancestral line, the nobility you can find on the family tree.

Now the next six words. Our discussion kept them germane to a planning situation we often find in the daily news: testing a nuclear power plant. Do you remember the words and their slight variations in meaning?

> We said the engineers had to consider every *contingency,* everything that might happen, to avoid an *emergency,* an unexpected occurrence that usually leads to the need for immediate ac-

tion, an *exigency*. Once the *crisis*, the turning point, is passed, the engineers know they probably won't have to worry about *extricating* themselves from *dire straits*.

Whew! You may feel pressure, *exigency*, in a situation that *strait*, that difficult. By the way, *strait* may relate to the names of narrow bodies of water connecting larger bodies of water—like the *Straits* of Mackinaw, between Lake Michigan and Lake Huron.

You may have avoided using the next group of words because you were unsure of them.

If you are an *anesthetist*, trained in the use of *anesthetics*, but not a doctor, you administer an *anesthetic* to cause *anesthesia*, a loss of feeling.

A doctor who specializes in the science of *anesthesia* is an *anesthesiologist*.

The next few words really dealt more with pronunciations and plural formations than meanings, so please try pronouncing the words with the preferred singular and plural. How about *data* and *status*?

The preferred pronunciations are still *dāta* and *stātus*, and one more—*strāta*—with a long *a*.

The singulars of *data* and *strata* end in *um*. So, it's *datum* or *data*, meaning "facts," "information." Common usage indicates that *data* will soon be approved as singular also.

The same is true of *stratum/strata*, meaning "layer or layers" and *criterion/criteria*, meaning "standard or standards for judgment or evaluation." *Status* adds *es* for the plural and means "condition" or "rank," like unmarried *status* or improving his *status*, his prestige.

The other three groups we included in our discussion of pronunciation and singular and plural endings began with the word that means an "observable fact or event," something that happens. What is it?

Phenomenon, singular, and *phenomena,* plural. The adjective is *phenomenal,* meaning "extraordinary," "very special," "remarkable." A total eclipse is an impressive *phenomenon* to watch.

What is the word meaning a branched candle holder or lamp?

That's *candelabrum* for the singular and *candelabra* for plural. However, since the early nineteenth century, *candelabra* has been accepted as singular, with the accepted plural *candelabras.*

The other word we mentioned using the formerly plural *a* ending for the singular is *agenda.*

Agendas can be used for the plural, and they're the plans, the organization of events, you make before you try to conduct a meeting. An *agenda* is a schedule, a sequence to keep a meeting on the track.

If you had given all those *succinct* explanations, we'd say you had done very well in avoiding *extraneous* thoughts. You would, indeed, be a *paragon* to *emulate*! (If you don't remember the words in this paragraph, return to Section I.)

Now it's time to complete Exercises 3 and 4 and Pretest 3.

EXERCISE 3

Directions: Fill in each blank in the following paragraph with one of the following words:

anesthetic   anesthesia   anesthetist   anesthesiologist
data   status   stratum
candelabra   criterion   phenomenon   agenda

Nurse Jones had spent a year studying to be an (1) _____. She works under the guidance of an (2) _____. Jones administers the (3) _____, but she is not permitted to verify if a state of (4) _____ is present in the patient. She reads the (5) _____ on the tape from the monitoring equipment. Last year she helped establish a (6) _____ or norm to determine when the patient is truly unconscious. The single (7) _____ of shut eyes is certainly not sufficient. Nurse Jones takes pride in the fact that each day she has a clear format in readiness. The doctor knows immediately by looking at her (8) _____ just what has to be done first. She carefully notes the (9) _____ of everyone in the operating room, what duty is assigned to each person, and the level or (10) _____ for which training has been completed. Nurse Jones allows herself one eccentricity: when she returns home from work, she turns on no lights; she lights one silver (11) _____ and relaxes in its glow.

EXERCISE 4

Directions: On the lines in the following sentences, write the words in parentheses that *best fit the meanings* of the sentences.

1. Some nurses have difficulty in administering _____ (*anesthesia, anesthetic*).
2. A person who is always concerned about his _____ (*status, strata*) in life watches what others are doing, buying, or earning.
3. When the patient began to awaken before the prescribed time, the surgeon made a hasty call for the _____ (*anesthesiologist, anesthesia*).
4. Home computers allow the average person to store much more _____ (*data, strata*) than ever before.
5. The _____ (*anesthetist, anesthetic*) has the responsibility for making the patient unconscious.
6. Liberace was famous for having one _____ (*candelabra, candelabrum*) on his piano.
7. Each _____ (*stratum, strata*) of the inner earth fascinates the world of science.
8. The _____ (*criteria, phenomena*) for entrance into the U.S. military academies are many and varied.
9. When the manager follows his _____ (*datum, agenda*) at monthly meetings, there is little discord.
10. Halley's comet is a _____ (*phenomenon, phenomena*) that occurs once every seventy-six years.
11. In acupuncture, a state of _____ (*anesthesia, anesthetic*) is not considered necessary.

Pretest 3

Directions: Match the meanings in column A with the
words in column B. On the line, write the word from
column B that *is closest in meaning*.

A	B
1. speak in opposition _____	circumference
2. false science _____	circumlocution
3. false indication _____	circumvent
4. inferior in rank _____	circumnavigate
5. prudent, correct _____	circumspect
6. to go around, avoid _____	contraindication
7. symptoms similar to	
tuberculosis _____	contradict
8. underground _____	pseudoscience
9. sail around, bypass _____	pseudopregnancy
10. distance around a circle _____	pseudotuberculosis
11. talking around the point _____	subordinate
12. false pregnancy _____	subterranean

Secton II, List 3

Let's talk about a few more prefixes. You who are so erudite
undoubtedly remember the nine we discussed in Section I:

> *ab, ad*
> *com* or *con*
> *de*, *ex*, *in*
> *pre*, *pro*, and *re*

Now let's introduce some new prefixes. The first two
begin with *c*. We had *com* or *con*, meaning "with,"
"together." *Circum* means "around," "about." One exam-

ple is the word *circumference*, meaning the "distance around a circle." Can you think of others?

> *Circumlocution* means to "talk around with too many words" or "talk around the point to avoid it," to be "evasive."

> Then there's *circumvent*, to "go around" or "avoid," as in *circumventing* customs with diplomatic passports.

> *Circumnavigate* means to "sail around" and also to "bypass," as in circumnavigating a congested area.

> *Circumspect* literally means "looking around," but it has been stretched to include "considering possible consequences carefully." It translates as "prudent," "wise."

Then we have *contradiction*, *contraindication*, and *contrary*. Yes, *contra* is another prefix beginning with a *c*. *Contra* means "against," "opposite," or "contrasting." It's common, and remembering what it means will help you figure out the meanings of new words.

> *Contraindication* means an "opposite indication." It often refers to an indication that makes using a procedure inadvisable, as in medicines that might produce an undesirable reaction.

> *Contradict* means to "speak in opposition"—it even implies correcting what has been said or denying it.

> *Contrary* means "opposite," as in *contrary* to common belief.

How about a *d* prefix, *dis*? You undoubtedly know *dis*approve and *dis*agree and *dis*able. From those words, you can deduce that the *dis* prefix means about the same as the prefix *un*. All those *dis* words mean "not approve," "not agree," and "not able." What's the difference between the meanings of *un* and *dis*?

There are several prefixes that mean *not*, that denote the negative. We've had *in*, but others are *il*, as in *il*legal; *im*, as in *im*pair; *in*, as in *in*decent; and *ir*, as in *ir*rational. They all have Latin roots and are customarily used with some words and not with others. A good dictionary may be necessary to know which to add to the root word, but there are some general guidelines to help you.

Usually *il* is used before words beginning with:

> *l, illegitimate*

The prefix *im* is used before words beginning with:

> *b, imbalance*
>
> *m, immoral*
>
> *p, improper*

Ir is used before words beginning with:

> *r, irregular*

In or *un* are used with the rest.

Webster's Ninth New Collegiate Dictionary lists almost two pages of words beginning with the prefix *un*.

Now let's go back to the original negative we mentioned, *dis*. It has a slightly different meaning.

Dictionaries give the meanings of *dis* as "away" (as *disbelief* being "away from belief") and "opposite" (*discourteous* being the opposite of "courteous") and as differing from simply not believing or not being courteous. However, the line is a fine one, so it's back to the dictionary.

There are two more common prefixes to look at now. The first is *pseudo,* as in *pseudonym* and *pseudointellectual.* From those two words you might speculate that the prefix *pseudo* means "fake"; you'd be correct. The dictionary defines it as "false." Those two words mean a false name and a false intellectual. *Pseudo* also adds the idea of being apparently rather than actually true.

Pseudoscience is a system of theories, assumptions, and methods erroneously regarded as science.

Pseudopregnancy and *pseudotuberculosis* have many of the characteristics of pregnancy and tuberculosis but aren't.

Let's look at the prefix *sub.* You may think of *subway* meaning an "underground train or passageway," *subterranean* meaning "underground," and *subfreezing* meaning "below freezing." In those, *sub* seems to mean "under," "below." But does it *always* mean "under" or "below"?

It's certainly a commonly used prefix, but no, it doesn't always mean physically "under" or "below."

Let's look at some of the nuances. Can you think of a word when the prefix *sub* means any of the following:

A lower position or rank? *Subeditor* is one.

A portion of? How about *subdivision*?

Less than perfect? *Substandard.*

Almost or nearly? *Subteen.*

Falling nearly in the category or bordering on? *Subarctic.*

You could say—somewhat loosely—that all of these words mean "below" or "under." But, as you see, the words using the *sub* prefix go beyond those two meanings.

Now complete Exercises 5 and 6 and Pretest 4 before we continue.

EXERCISE 5

Directions: On each line, write the *prefix* that means *not* that can be used to make the following words negative.

1. _____ regular		6. _____ possible
2. _____ proper		7. _____ logical
3. _____ legal		8. _____ mobile
4. _____ balance		9. _____ courteous
5. _____ moral		10. _____ religious

EXERCISE 6

Directions: On the lines in the following sentences, write the words in parentheses that *best fit the meanings* of the sentences.

1. The members of the historical society were told that there would be time for questions provided there were no _____ (*circumlocutions, circumferences*) to waste time.

2. The tardy _____ (*circumspect, subordinate*) was looked upon with disdain by his employer.

3. The _____ (*circumference, contraindication*) of the table at the European meeting of NATO officials became a paramount issue.

4. The doctor told the young woman that the cure she was taking was the result of _____ (*pseudoscience, pseudopregnancy*) rather than valid research.

5. The policeman told the tourist to take an alternate route to _____ (*contradict, circumvent*) the heavy city traffic.

6. Even when she noticed the symptoms of rapidly increasing weight and appetite, the doctor assured the young woman that she was experiencing _____ (*pseudotuberculosis, pseudopregnancy*).

7. Columbus felt he could _____ (*circumference, circumnavigate*) the land mass before him.

8. _____ (*Pseudotuberculosis, Pseudoscience*) was more prevalent in the coal-mining towns than in the shore communities.

9. If you _____ (*contradict, circumvent*) others only when necessary and avoid a show of superior knowledge, your friendships will be stronger.

10. The football official threw his penalty flag on the ground and then picked it up. This _____ (*circumlocution, contraindication*) of messages angered the fans who were unable to determine the status of the play.

11. A carefully _____ (*circumspect, subordinate*) attitude is best when traveling in a new city.

Pretest 4

Directions: Match the meanings in column A with the words in column B. On the line, write the word from column B that is *closest in meaning*.

A	B
1. abstention _____	worldly
2. consummate (verb) _____	science of order of nature
3. consummate (adj) _____	everywhere present
4. cosmopolitan _____	laughable, ridiculous
5. cosmopolite _____	summary, list
6. cosmic _____	worldly person
7. cosmography _____	voluntarily refraining
8. malapropism _____	confuse
9. ubiquitous _____	bring to completion
10. compendium _____	misuse of words
11. ludicrous _____	relating to the universe
12. obfuscate _____	complete, perfect

Section II, List 4

Let's see if prefixes have helped you when you meet new words. You've already speculated on the meanings for words in the Pretest. Do you want to gamble on the word *abstention*?

Your line of reasoning might go like this: "The prefix *ab* means 'from' or 'away.' I don't know the rest, but I'd guess 'stay away.' I bet it's related to *abstain*, and when congressmen *abstain*, they hold back from voting. So *abstention* must mean 'holding back from doing something.' "

If that was your thought process, you'd win that bet!

Abstention does indeed mean the "act of abstaining," "refraining deliberately." The noun *abstinence* means "voluntarily refraining from indulgence in food or drink" and may involve an act of strong self-denial, as in dieting.

You may have a question about the word beginning with the prefix *con*. You hear it pronounced with the accent on both the first and second syllables—*con*summate and con*sum*mate. Which is correct?

Both. But let's look at the word. The prefix *con* has the same meaning as *com*: "with," "together." You might associate *sum* with "adding together," and you'd be correct. However, there are complications.

> The verb *cońsummāte*—with the accent on the first syllable and the long *a*—means to "bring to completion," to "complete," "finish," as to *consummate* a merger.

> In marriage, *consummate* means to "complete the wedding vows by sexual intercourse."

> We also have *cońsummātor* and *cońsummătive*, with the accent on the first syllable.

> But the adjective shifts the accent. We have *consúmmate*, meaning "complete," "perfect," "100 percent." He seemed to be the *consúmmate* Easterner, or he was a *consúmmate* politician. The accent is on the second syllable, and the *a* sounds like a short *i*.

You really have to know how the word is being used to know how to pronounce it.

Another pair of related words with a shifting accent is *cosmopólitan* and *cosmopolite*.

Cosmopolitan, an adjective meaning "worldwide," "not limited to one area," "worldly," has the accent on *pol*.

Cosmopolitan may describe something like herbs that are found worldwide or subjects of worldwide interest, of *cosmopolitan* appeal.

The noun is *cosmopolite*, with the accent on the *mop*. It may refer to people who are at home anywhere in the world, members of the so-called jet set.

From the same root, we have *cosmic*, relating to the universe, and *cosmonaut*, one who travels beyond the earth's atmosphere.

There are other members of this interesting family.

Less frequently used are *cosmography*, the science that deals with the order of nature, and *cosmographer*, the person who specializes in that science. Geology, geography, and astronomy are branches of *cosmography*. In both of those words, the accent is on *mog*.

One reason for the shift, of course, is pronunciation. The accent on the first syllable leaves you with an awkward pronunciation, except in the word *cosmopolitan*, when we accent both *cos* and *pol*. You don't need any more details, but you do need to be aware of that shifting accent.

Now let's examine another sentence:

We'll look at a few *malapropisms* that seem to be *ubiquitous* in our world and provide a *compendium* of *ludicrously* misused words that serve to *obfuscate* rather than to elucidate.

You say that's too many long and difficult words? *Malapropisms* often include too many long and difficult words. Mrs. Malaprop used them in the wrong places, in place of words that sounded similar. She was a character in Richard Sheridan's 1775 play, *The Rivals*. Mrs. Malaprop continually mangled the language.

Few of us are familiar with the play or any of the other characters, but the terms *malaprop* and *malapropism* have been used to describe not only the wrong use of individual words but also mixed quotations.

Malapropisms have been the foundation of comedy acts ever since Mrs. Malaprop's debut. In fact, before her, there were the clownish "fools" from Shakespeare's plays. They, too, misused words for comic effect.

However, misusing words when laughter isn't your goal can give a very undesirable image of *you*.

Let's work through our sentence. It really was anomalous. We believe communications should be succinct and lucid.

The first word was *ubiquitous*. You probably won't find any relatives to that word in your vocabulary. It comes from the Latin *ubique*, meaning "everywhere."

Ubiquity, the noun, means "presence everywhere," and the adverb is *ubiquitously*. You may hear the noun *ubiquitousness*.

The adjective in the original sentence, *ubiquitous*, means "existing everywhere at the same time," "constantly encountered," "widespread." You may read in the newspapers about a discussion of the

military budget being *ubiquitous* or of the *ubiquity*
of poverty in Africa.

The next word was *compendium*. We used it in a slight
variation of the usual meaning—but one listed in *Webster's*.
Usually *compendium* means a "brief summary of a larger
work." You, of course, were aware of the prefix *com*, so
you could get the idea of "being together."

The adjective *compendious* is a synonym for
"concise."

Another variation is the one we used: a "list of
items" or a "collection." We said a *compendium*
of *ludicrously* misused words—a list or collection
of misused words.

Then there's *ludicrously*. *Ludicrous* means "humorous,"
"laughable," "amusing." It may include exaggeration,
absurdity, or some incongruity, but the result is laughable.
And *obfuscate*? Speculate. Can you think of another word
that looks similar? How about *obstruct*? At least it begins
with *ob*. You might speculate that it means to "obstruct" in
some way. Since we used it as the opposite of "elucidate,"
you might guess it means to "obstruct the meaning rather
than make it clear." If you did follow that line of reasoning,
you'd be correct.

Obfuscate literally means to "darken," to "obscure." We use it to mean to "confuse." The
noun is *obfuscation*, and the adjective *obfuscatory*.

The adjective shifts the accent from *ob* to *fus*. The
change in accent makes pronunciation much easier.

Now you can see how *malapropisms* can, indeed, be *obfuscatory* and lead to a *compendium* of *ludicrously* misused words.

That's quite a difficult list. Let's review them—quickly.

First we had to *abstain*, to refrain from doing something like eating food not on our diet.

Then came *cońsummāte*, the verb meaning to "complete" or "finish," and *consúmmate*, the adjective meaning "complete," "perfect," "100 percent."

Cosmopólitan is an adjective meaning "worldly," "at home anywhere," and *cosmópolite* the noun meaning "one who is *cosmopolitan*." That's often associated with the rich and sophisticated.

Then the *malapropism* sentence. (Remember, Mrs. Malaprop was a character in a play who slaughtered English by using words in the wrong places or the right places with wrong meanings.)

That practice is now *malapropism*—small *m*, by the way.

The sentence included *ubiquitous*, meaning "everywhere."

Compendium means a "summary" but can also mean a "list" or "collection."

In the case of malapropisms, it may be a collection of *ludicrous* or funny lines, lines that *obfuscate* or obscure meaning rather than make it clear.

Now, please complete Exercises 7 and 8 and Pretest 5. After Pretest 5, we'll share some malapropisms.

EXERCISE 7

Directions: On the lines in the following sentences, write
the words in parentheses that *best fit the meanings* of the
sentences.

Not wanting to (1) _____ (*obfuscate, ludicrous*) the
issue, I want to point out that there are two ways of
pronouncing the name of Halley, the man responsible for the
name of the comet that visits our (2) _____ (*cosmos,
cosmography*) about every seventy-six years. The preferred
pronunciation rhymes with "valley." It would be (3)
_____ (*ludicrous, cosmopolitan*) to insist upon associating the (4) _____ (*cosmopolitan, ludicrous*) as-
tronomer with the rock group known as Bill Haley and the
Comets. This kind of association probably accounts for
many confused uses, many (5) _____ (*malapropisms,
cosmopolites*), by careless speakers. In 1682, using his own
home telescope, the (6) _____ (*cosmographer, ubiquitous*) Halley first saw what would eventually carry his
name. This led him on a pilgrimage to Sir Isaac Newton,
the most (7) _____ (*consummate, ludicrous*) of English scientists. The gregarious Halley was one of the few
men the austere Newton would see in person. Newton said
he was aware of the phenomenon and even had calculations
on it somewhere in his study. Halley prevailed upon Newton
to have his (8) _____ (*cosmos, compendium*) printed.
Newton favored _____ (*abstention, malapropisms*)
but eventually agreed. When he did (10) _____
(*consummate, obfuscate*) the total work, it became *The
Mathematical Principles of Natural Philosophy,* a study that
not only explained the motion of comets but revolutionized
our conception of the (11) _____ (*ludicrous, cosmic*)
extent of our orderly universe.

EXERCISE 8

Directions: Match the words in column A with the meanings in column B. On the line, write the word from
column B that is *closest in meaning*.

	A		B
1.	confusion _____	ludicrous
2.	concise _____	cosmic
3.	person bored by too much worldly experience _____	malapropisms
4.	relating to the universe, vast ___	abstain
5.	bring to a desired conclusion ___	compendious
6.	laughable _____	cosmopolite
7.	confusion of words and phrases _____	consummate (adj.)
8.	voluntarily refrain from _____	cosmos
9.	the ultimate, perfect _____	obfuscation
10.	acquainted with the wonders of the world _____	cosmography
11.	the orderly system of the universe _____	cosmopolitan
12.	the science dealing with the order of nature and the universe _____	consummate (verb)

Pretest 5

Directions: Match the meanings in column A with the words in column B. On the line, write the word from column B that *is closest in meaning*.

A		B
1. understand	_____	progeny
2. common language	_____	prodigy
3. tombstone inscription	_____	reprehend
4. descendants	_____	comprehend
5. delete from print	_____	oracular
6. a reprimand	_____	vernacular
7. photoelectric cell	_____	deranged
8. omen, bright child	_____	epitaph
9. descriptive phrase, profanity	_____	epithet
10. steady, uniform	_____	censor
11. study of insects	_____	censure
12. study of words	_____	censer
13. authoritative	_____	sensor
14. incense burner	_____	equable
15. to criticize	_____	equitable
16. fair, just	_____	entomology
17. disturbed	_____	etymology

Section II, List 5

Now for some malapropisms, some of the lady's own. She describes a person as a "*progeny* of learning" and mystifies everyone around her with this sentence defending her own use of language:

> "Sure, if I *reprehend* anything in the world, it is the use of my *oracular* tongue and a nice *derangement* of *epitaphs*."

No wonder her name became associated with confusing misuse!

You undoubtedly know that *progeny* means "descendants," "children." You also are used to seeing it used as a plural noun. Apparently Mrs. M. had it confused with *prodigy*, a word describing a highly talented or bright child.

Interestingly, *prodigy* comes from a Latin word meaning "omen" or "monster." It's still used occasionally to mean an "omen" or "portentous event." In fact, that's the first meaning given in *Webster's*. The way you probably hear *prodigy* used most often, the third and last meaning, is in reference to a talented child.

What about those other choice words of Mrs. M's? *Reprehend* was one. You may remember thinking she must mean *comprehend*, which means to "grasp the nature, significance, or meaning of"—to "understand." And you're right.

> To *reprehend* means to "voice disapproval of," to "criticize." We also have the adjective *reprehensible*, meaning "deserving criticism," and the noun *reprehension*, meaning "censure."

That word *censure* is one we'll talk about later, but let's finish the sentence we started.

The sentence was, "If I *reprehend* anything in the world, it is the use of my *oracular* tongue and a nice *derangement* of *epitaphs*."

What do you think she meant by "*oracular* tongue"?
It sounds like it would be associated with *oracle*, a person, priestess, or ancient Greek through whom the gods spoke. People used to go to *oracles* to get answers to weighty questions or to receive predictions of the future.

> Continuing with that line of thought, *oracular* is used to mean "resembling an *oracle*" as in solemn delivery. The usual synonyms are "dictatorial," "authoritative."

The lady may have meant *vernacular*—using the language or dialect of a region, usually of the common natives. Probably she was referring to the use of her native tongue, but she was trying to sound less "common."

She probably also meant *arrangement* of epitaphs rather than *derangement*. Using the prefix *de*—meaning "from," "away from"—means "disarranged," not "arranged." In fact, *deranged* even means "mentally disturbed" and "insane."

What of *epitaphs*? Was she proud of her use of her native language and an arrangement of inscriptions on tombs? That's very doubtful. Probably she had in mind the word *epithet*, which has two rather different meanings, one classical and one modern. The classical one, and the one she probably meant, is a stock adjective or descriptive phrase for use in similar situations when describing the same person or similar people. Here are some examples of *epithets*:

> "The Great Emancipator" as a name for Abraham Lincoln

"The Babe" for George Herman Ruth
"The Swedish Nightingale" for singer Jenny Lind

You may associate the word *epithet* with profanity. You may remember seeing in magazine interviews, for example, the phrase "*epithet* deleted" and thought that meant they took out the swear word. If so, score a point for a good memory.

> Using *epithet* to mean "profanity" or "obscenity" is a very recent use and is still officially disliked—especially by those who know the classical meaning. It is, however, generally considered established and acceptable. In communicating with a hairsplitter, you do run the risk of being censured. It may be that it's confused with *expletive*, too.

We mentioned that we wanted to say something about *censure*. It is one of four words that sound alike, that are pronounced very nearly alike by most people. Do you know them?

First, there's the verb *censor*.

> It's a word we know if we get mail from countries where the government doesn't believe in freedom for individuals writing to others who are out of the country. We sometimes have attempts at *censoring* here in the United States when a group decides to delete portions of films or books for moral or political reasons.

The person who does the *censoring* is a *censor*, a noun, spelled the same way.

No, that doesn't count as the second of the four! There are four spellings with similar pronunciations.

The second one is *censure* and it means to "criticize severely."

> It's usually done by a group of people such as lawyers who *censure* a colleague's professional behavior.

> *Censure* often has the connotation of being at least a semiofficial reprimand.

It's pronounced with the *s* having the sound of *sh,* as if it were spelled sen*sh*ure.

The third one is pronounced exactly like *censor,* as in censoring the mail, but the spelling differs. It's c-e-n-s-e-r and means an "incense burner," especially one suspended by chains and used in a religious ceremony.

> In the Roman and Anglican Catholic churches, for example, incense is a part of the celebration of holy days, and the *censer* contains the burning incense.

So we have a *censor,* who removes portions of books and letters that he considers unacceptable; he *censors* them. A *censure* is a reprimand for individuals not adhering to codes for their professions. A *censer* is a container for incense.

The fourth word you see in technical articles and science fiction is *sensor,* which refers to a cell that responds to a stimulus. Robots have *sensors* to warn them when they approach another object. That similar pronunciation can cause lots of confusion.

We'll look at just two more pairs, words all beginning with the letter *e.* Then we'll go to suffixes.

The first word is *equable*, which means "uniform," "lacking any noticeable extreme," "steady."

> Several surveys of public opinion may produce *equable* results.

Equable is often confused with *equitable*. In fact, they rank high on any list of frequently "Webstered" words— words frequently sought in a dictionary.

> *Equitable* means "fair," "equal," "having *equity*," the noun meaning "justice," "freedom from bias."

> You often hear of *equable* agreements or rules when the speaker really means "fair and just," not "steady."

The other two *e* words are *entomology* and *etymology*. Do you keep them straight? They're each the science of or the knowledge about something, but one is of insects and the other of words. You think of *n*'s to keep them clear.

> *Entomology*—beginning with *en*—is the study of insects.

> The study of words is called *etymology*—no *n*, and with a *y* before the *m*. The people who do these studies are *entomologists* and *etymologists*, respectively.

Let's go back over the last eighteen words. Many are pairs, so it isn't quite the overload it appears to be. We began by discussing *malapropisms*. They led us to *progeny* and *prodigy*.

Progeny means "children, descendants."

Prodigy has three meanings: an "omen or portent," "something extraordinary or inexplicable," and—based on its Latin ancestor meaning a "monster"—a "talented child."

The next word was *reprehend*, which Mrs. Malaprop confused with *comprehend*.

Reprehend means "criticize," "disapprove of," and *reprehensible* means "deserving that criticism."

Reprehension means "severe criticism or judgment."

To *comprehend* is to "understand."

How about *oracular*? You associate that with those ancient oracles who gave all the answers, and the word means "authoritative," since they were authorities on all subjects.

Vernacular means a "manner of expression of a certain group," often opposed to the literary or cultured who try not to speak in the *vernacular*.

Arranged means "order," and *deranged* means "disorder," even "insanity."
And *epitaph* and *epithet*?

The first one is easy: *epitaphs* are words carved on gravestones.

An *epithet* originally was a descriptive word or phrase used as a standard description. It might even become part of the person's name in the minds of many. The modern trend is to also use it to mean "profanity" or "obscenity."

Let's go on to *censor*, *censure*, *censer*, and *sensor*.

To *censor* is to delete material from a letter or play or book because of some established standard. The *censor*, spelled and pronounced the same way, does the *censoring*—banning a play because some find it offensive, for example.

Censure is pronounced as if it were cen*sh*ure and means to "criticize," "condemn," or "reprimand" —as in *censuring* a company contractor for taking bribes.

The last one beginning with a *c*, *censer*, means "incense holder."

The fourth one, *sensor*, refers to cells that respond to stimuli.

The last two pairs are easy:

Equable means "steady," "uniform"—as in *equable* survey results.

Equitable means "fair," "just," "having *equity* or justice"—an *equitable* settlement of a strike.

And the last one: *entomology* and *etymology*. Remember the letter *n*.

Entomology is the science or study of insects, and *etymology* is the science or knowledge of words.

It is now time to complete Exercises 9 and 10 and Pretest 6.

EXERCISE 9

Directions: On the lines in the following sentences, write the words in parentheses that *best fit the meanings* of the sentences.

1. Einstein is an excellent example of a child not considered a _____ (*prodigy, progeny*) but certainly possessing extraordinary abilities.

2. The schoolmaster in the story began treating the main character with _____ (*reprehension, censer*) as soon as he saw the paper airplane sail out the window.

3. An altar boy who tends the _____ (*censer, censor*) at Eastertime feels honored by the trust placed in him.

4. During wartime there is a need to _____ (*censor, censure*) mail; even a small remark about a destination could aid the enemy.

5. Sadly, the films and stage productions of today contain many more _____ (*epitaphs, epithets*) than those of former times.

6. The settlement finally agreed upon was clearly not _____ (*equable, equitable*) to the groups not represented by the committee.

7. The king made the mistake of thinking his _____ (*prodigy, progeny*) would be as charitable as he had always been with his possessions.

8. The pompous judge spoke in _____ (an *oracular*, a *vernacular*) manner.

9. If you _____ (*censure, censer*) your children from morning till night, they will never have a chance to demonstrate responsibility on their own.

10. That survey company has established a reputation of providing consistently _____ (*equable, equitable*) statistics.

11. One of the most famous _____ (*epitaphs, epithets*) is on Shakespeare's tomb in Stratford-on-Avon.

12. A gifted speaker is not afraid of occasional _____ (*vernacular, progeny*) expressions in his speeches; in fact, he may purposely include them.

13. On a test that may decide your future, the first step is to be certain you _____ (*reprehend, comprehend*) the instructions.

14. That study of insects in high school captured his interest and resulted in a long career in _____ (*etymology, entomology*).

15. The photoelectric cell responded as a _____ (*censer, sensor*) should.

16. The complete _____ (*arrangement, derangement*) of the store window suggested an internal explosion.

17. The _____ (*etymologist, entomologist*) treated individual words as members of his living family.

EXERCISE 10

Directions: Match the words in column A with the meanings in column B. On the line, write the word from column B that is *closest in meaning*.

A	B
1. censor _____	understand
2. progeny _____	common language
3. prodigy _____	tombstone inscription
4. censure _____	descendants
5. epithet _____	delete as from print
6. equable _____	reprimand
7. censer _____	photoelectric cell
8. epitaph _____	omen, bright child
9. reprehend _____	descriptive phrase, profanity
10. oracular _____	steady, uniform
11. deranged _____	study of insects
12. equitable _____	study of words
13. comprehend _____	authoritative
14. entomology _____	incense burner
15. sensor _____	criticize
16. etymology _____	fair, just
17. vernacular _____	disturbed

Pretest 6

Directions: On the line following it, write the meaning of each suffix.

1. –logy _____
2. –ly _____
3. –ful _____
4. –ship _____
5. –like _____

Section II, List 6

Let's look at those suffixes. We've already used *logy*, meaning "science" or "theory" of something. *Sociology* is the science of society, *zoology* is the science of animals, and *biology* is the branch of knowledge that deals with living organisms. The *logy* suffix often implies the study of that science, also, as we saw with *anesthesiologist*.

How about the simple suffix *ly*, as in *womanly* or *briefly*? The suffix itself means "like." It's used to change nouns into descriptive words, adjectives.

Changing *woman* to *womanly* alters the noun to an adjective meaning "like a woman" or "having the characteristics of a woman." We speak of *womanly* graces—graces characteristic of a woman—for example.

We also use *ly* on the ends of adjectives to make them adverbs for describing verbs, adjectives, and other adverbs. So the adjective *brief* to describe a speech becomes *briefly* to describe how long the speaker spoke.

Other suffixes that do much the same thing are *ful*, *ship*, and *like*.

> *Beautiful* means "characteristic of beauty"; *friendship* means "characteristic of friends"; *sportsmanlike* means "characteristic of a good sportsman."

> *Ful* may also mean "full of" as in *spoonful* or *plentiful*.

How about a quick run through suffixes?

> *Logy* means "science" or "knowledge," as *entomology* being the knowledge of insects.

> *Ly* means "like" and is used to change nouns to adjectives (*woman* to *womanly*) and to change adjectives to adverbs (*brief* to *briefly*).

> Then *ful*, *ship*, and *like*, mean "characteristic of." Examples are *beautiful*, *friendship*, and *sportsmanlike*. *Ful* can also make "full of," as in *spoonful*.

In Section I, we introduced—or at least discussed—fifty words and nine prefixes. In Section II, we've reviewed thirteen of those words and introduced fifty more. We've also talked about six more prefixes and five suffixes.

How far do we have to go? How many words are there in the English language? Good questions; fuzzy answer. No one knows how many there are. One *official* estimate is eight hundred thousand but the number is constantly changing. About two hundred thousand new ones have come into acceptable use in the past decade. We'll be talking about some of them in the next section. And, no, we aren't planning to look at quite all eight hundred thousand! Right now, concentrate on the hundred-plus that we've shared, and complete Exercise 11.

EXERCISE 11

Directions: On the lines, write the proper suffixes to the following words to *best fit the meanings* of the sentences.

1. The woman was everything you desire aesthetically; she was beauti_____.
2. The science of society is known as socio_____.
3. His manner of dialogue was characterized by brevity; he always spoke brief_____.
4. I suppose every father would like to instill a sports-man_____ attitude in his children.
5. Friend_____ includes all connotations of being a friend.

Pretest 1	Exercise 1	Exercise 2
1. aptitude for making fortunate discoveries	1. ability to find the unexpected	1. serendipity
2. ancestral line	2. ancestral line	2. pedigree
3. urgency	3. urgency	3. emergency
4. unexpected occurrence needing action	4. unexpected occurrence	4. a contingency
5. possibility	5. possible option	5. extricate
6. turning point	6. turning point	6. crisis
7. desperate	7. desperate	7. dire
8. tight place, narrow passage	8. tight place, narrow passage	8. straits
9. untangle, free	9. untangle	9. exigency

Pretest 2

1. status
2. criterion
3. anesthetic
4. candelabra
5. anesthesiologist
6. stratum
7. data
8. phenomenon
9. anesthetist
10. anesthesiology
11. agenda

Exercise 3

1. anesthetist
2. anesthesiologist
3. anesthetic
4. anesthesia
5. data
6. criterion
7. phenomenon
8. agenda
9. status
10. stratum
11. candelabra

Exercise 4

1. anesthetic
2. status
3. anesthesiologist
4. data
5. anesthetist
6. candelabra
7. stratum
8. criteria
9. agenda
10. phenomenon
11. anesthesia

Pretest 3

1. contradict
2. pseudoscience
3. contraindication
4. subordinate
5. circumspect
6. circumvent
7. pseudo-tuberculosis
8. subterranean
9. circumnavigate
10. circumference
11. circumlocution
12. pseudopregnancy

Exercise 5

1. irregular
2. improper
3. illegal
4. imbalance
5. immoral
6. impossible
7. illogical
8. immobile
9. discourteous
10. irreligious

Exercise 6

1. circumlocutions
2. subordinate
3. circumference
4. pseudoscience
5. circumvent
6. pseudopregnancy
7. circumnavigate
8. pseudo-tuberculosis
9. contradict
10. contraindication
11. circumspect

Pretest 4

1. voluntarily refraining
2. bring to completion
3. complete, perfect
4. worldly
5. worldly person
6. relating to the universe
7. science of order of nature
8. misuse of words
9. everywhere present
10. summary, list
11. laughable, ridiculous
12. confuse

Exercise 7

1. obfuscate
2. cosmos
3. ludicrous
4. cosmopolitan
5. malapropisms
6. cosmographer
7. consummate
8. compendium
9. abstention
10. consummate
11. cosmic

Exercise 8

1. obfuscation
2. compendious
3. cosmopolite
4. cosmic
5. consummate (verb)
6. ludicrous
7. malapropisms
8. abstain
9. consummate (adj.)
10. cosmopolitan
11. cosmos
12. cosmography

Pretest 5

1. comprehend
2. vernacular
3. epitaph
4. progeny
5. censor
6. censure
7. sensor
8. prodigy
9. epithet
10. equable
11. entomology
12. etymology
13. oracular
14. censer
15. reprehend
16. equitable
17. deranged

Exercise 9

1. prodigy
2. reprehension
3. censer
4. censor
5. epithets
6. equitable
7. progeny
8. an oracular
9. censure
10. equable
11. epitaphs
12. vernacular
13. comprehend
14. entomology
15. sensor
16. derangement
17. etymologist

Exercise 10

1. delete as from print
2. descendants
3. omen, bright child
4. reprimand
5. descriptive phrase, profanity
6. steady, uniform
7. incense burner
8. tombstone inscription
9. criticize
10. authoritative
11. disturbed
12. fair, just
13. understand
14. study of insects
15. photoelectric cell
16. study of words
17. common language

Pretest 6

1. science or theory of
2. like
3. characteristic of
4. characteristic of
5. characteristic of

Exercise 11

1. ful
2. logy
3. ly
4. like
5. ship

SECTION III

Have you ever considered that good thinking goes with a good vocabulary?

We think in words and pictures. Research shows that we think—and dream—in color. None of those black-and-white images for the modern brain! But if we think in words and must use words to describe our mental pictures to others, the more precise our words, the clearer the picture we communicate.

English reputedly has the most complete range of variations of meaning of any language, but too many of us settle for common, too-often-used, tired terms instead of image-makers.

That's where we come in! We've talked of fine nuances, connotations, and synonyms. All of those really give your mental images some muscle, fill out the generalities.

Everyone—you, us, and those who hear our words—has three vocabularies of varying lengths. We have words we understand when we read them in context. We don't necessarily know the precise definition of each word, but each makes sense in combination with other words. Then we have a smaller vocabulary that we use in writing, when we have time to think and choose. Our smallest vocabulary is the one we use when speaking. That one is limited to words we can immediately recall and use with confidence.

It would be beneficial to increase our speaking vocabulary to the size of our reading vocabulary, but not many people achieve that goal. There are only so many William F. Buckleys and Edwin Newmans, who are known for their knowledge of words. A more practical goal is to continue to increase all three vocabularies so that we can send and receive precise, succinct messages—to eliminate the guesswork.

That takes interest, effort, and practice. Let's share some ideas about how to review the words we've discussed before we go on.

We may have introduced a word in its adjective form, describing a noun. But we also mentioned how variations of the same word could serve other roles. For example, we mentioned *anomalous*, the adjective meaning "unusual," "irregular." We used the noun *anomaly:* minutes of a meeting written in poetry form would be an *anomaly*. There's also an adjective, *anomalously*, meaning "irregularly," "unusually," "varying from the normal." Consider the following:

> The plural of the word *ox* is *anomalously* formed, illustrates *anomalousness*, and is an *anomalous* formation.

In other words, the plural of the word *ox, oxen,* is an irregularity, is irregularly formed, illustrates irregularity, and is an irregular formation.

We mean, then, that to be comfortable with the word, we have to know how many costumes it wears, how many roles it can play in organized English.

In Section I we mentioned four verbs. To review them, when we provide the verb, you provide any other forms of the word you can think of—other parts of speech.

Without getting too involved in grammatical construction, here's a quick fix:

> *Nouns* name things and tell us what they are. *Adjectives* describe them. *Verbs* tell us what they do. *Adverbs* tell us how they do whatever they do.

If I give you the verb *denote*, what can you add? You can add the other parts of speech formed from that verb. Let's look at some examples to show you this method of reviewing— and using—new words.

> The verb *denote* means, literally, to "mean." A meaning is a *denotation* (noun), and something that provides meaning can be described as being *denotative* (adjective).

> To *connote* means to "imply," to "suggest more than the exact meaning." That implication or suggestion is called a *connotation* (noun), and when my answer implies more than an exact meaning, it is called *connotative* (adjective). I answer *connotatively* (adverb).

Do you see what you're doing? You looked at each word from different viewpoints, examined it, and tested variations. You may get the picture of mentally handling the words to discover how you can manipulate them—as you would manipulate modeling clay. It's a mental hands-on experience. Now, please complete Pretest 1 for Section III. (See p. 146 for the correct answers to the tests and exercises in this section.)

Pretest 1

Directions: Match the meanings in column A with the words in column B. On the line, write the word from column B that *is closest in meaning*.

A	B
1. words that sound alike _____	literate
2. not understandable _____	illiterate
3. to speak clearly _____	legible
4. able to read/write _____	readable
5. opposite position _____	unreadable
6. not able to read/write; uncultured __	unintelligible
7. readable (as in handwriting) _____	homonyms
8. rambling _____	antonyms
9. words with opposite meanings ____	articulate (verb)
10. commonplace _____	antithesis
11. can't be read _____	abnegate
12. deny, renounce _____	discursive
13. interesting to read _____	banal

Section III, List 1

Adding a prefix—one of those negative ones we discussed—can make another form of the word or another word entirely. Do you know what *literate* means? It denotes being able to read and write, but the connotation is as commonly meant: being cultured as well as educated, depending on the context. It even includes being versed in literature. (You can tell they come from the same root.)

A *literary* organization would include those interested in literature, books, authors, and scholarship.

> A *literary* agent is one who helps authors get their creative endeavors published.
>
> If an author dies, a *literary* executor is the person entrusted with the management of his papers and unpublished works.
>
> If you are a member of the *literati,* you are one of a group of people interested in literature or the arts, things appreciated by the well educated. The *literati* would include the erudite.

After all those related words, the Latin root will be no surprise; it's *liter,* meaning "letter" or "literature."

Now add the prefix *il: illiterate.* That means "not able to read and write." You can guess the connotation also holds true: uneducated and, connotatively speaking, apparently crude, uncultured. It's even stretched to refer to violating approved patterns of speaking or writing about a particular field—as an *illiterate* in the field of nuclear power—or displaying behavior typical of one who is *illiterate.*

> A teenager might be heard saying, "She's so *illiterate* she just doesn't appreciate common courtesy!"

The speaker wouldn't be condemning anyone's ability to read; the comment is obviously a judgment about socially acceptable manners.

On the other side of the coin, *legible* means "capable of being read," so we also use it to mean "clear"—as in "can be read clearly."

> Have you noticed that my writing is very *legible*? I'm rather proud of its *legibility*. I've always written *legibly*.

The prefix *il* adds the meaning "not." *Illegible* means "not capable of being read," "not clear." It also adds the connotation of being unclear, as in unable to be understood as well as read.

Readable follows the same pattern. *Readable* means "able to be read," and it can be a synonym for *legible*. They're synonyms if you're just talking about the physical clarity of the formation of letters. However, *readable* has the connotation of "interesting to read."

> I may write *readably* and have you compliment me on my *readability* because you like the subject of my short stories rather than the clarity of my penmanship.

> My ability to write clearly and interestingly may render discussion of a complicated and difficult subject like physics *readable*.

Adding the prefix *un*, *unreadable* may mean "unbearably dull and uninteresting." It might also refer to appropriateness: some jokes are not appropriate to read aloud in certain company—they're *unreadable* because of their content.

The fourth word-pair in this group is *intelligible* and *unintelligible*. *Intelligible* means "capable of being understood." It usually implies some intelligence. *Unintelligible* means "not only unclear but obscure and incomprehensible." As you can see, the negatives in that group included connotations that went further than the denotations, the exact meanings.

Now let's look at another learning aid, another method of permanently adding new words to your vocabulary. We'll use five words in the contexts of sentences. Speculate what each means. To do that, you may use *synonyms* or *homonyms* or *antonyms*.

As we discussed in Section I, *synonyms* are two or more words that have the same or similar meanings. We call them *synonymous*.

Are you familiar with *homonyms*? Those are words that sound alike but have different meanings. *Censor* and *censer* are *homonyms*.

Antonyms are words with opposite meanings: good and bad, up and down, in and out. That root *nym*, meaning "name," certainly gets around. We had *pseudonym*, meaning a "false name," too.

Our sentence said we could use *synonyms*, words meaning the same; *homonyms*, words sounding the same; and *antonyms*, words having opposite meanings, to speculate on the meanings of words in context. Let's look at what can be a very difficult sentence using the word *articulate*.

> She wasn't reluctant about *articulating* her criticism of how well he *articulated* each note of the

scale; in fact, she compared him to a certain *articulated* animal.

"*Articulating* her criticism" seems to refer to speaking up, voicing her criticism. "How well he *articulated* each note" might refer to how well he pronounced or sang each note. An "*articulated* animal" might be segmented, divided. Does that mean that these three words that sound alike but have different meanings are *homonyms*?

Not really. What looks and sounds like the same word does have three differing meanings, but they share a common root. Purists would not consider them *homonyms*. They all come from the Latin word meaning "jointed."

> When we use *articulate* as a verb meaning to "speak clearly" or to "utter an opinion effectively," we are referring to the clarity of the vocal expression, a clarity that leaves no room for misinterpretation.

> When we apply it to musical notes, the emphasis is on *articulating* each note clearly, breaking them distinctly—perhaps even dividing them into syllables.

> That brings us to an *articulated* animal. You can speculate on its meaning: "jointed" or "segmented."

The noun *articulation* means the "action or manner of jointing." It can also refer to the joints between bones or cartilages in the skeletons of vertebrates as well as to the act of uttering sounds. It refers broadly to clarity of sound and the coherent flow of speech.

There's an adjective that describes you when you express yourself clearly: *articulate*. It's spelled just like the verb but changes the pronunciation of the last syllable from *artículāte*, the verb, to *artículăte*, the adjective. The adverb, *artículătory*, means "distinctly" or "jointedly."

The more common word *article* is in this same family. An *article* is something that is distinct, can be identified as a particular one in a group. For example:

> We speak of *articles* in newspapers, *articles* of clothing, genuine *articles*, and so on.

Each can be identified as a portion, a segment, a particular item related to the general group—still going back to the idea of being joined to, a division of.

Here's another sentence to consider carefully, which uses the word *antithesis:*

> If communism is the *antithesis* of capitalism, the goals of the two philosophies are *antithetical*, the means of achieving them *antithetically* designed, and their slogans *antithetic*.

You may recognize a prefix we haven't mentioned: *anti*, meaning "against" or "opposite"—even "opposed." An *antithesis* must be the opposite of something else, may be opposed to it. The sentence says that communism is the opposite of capitalism, is anticapitalism.

What does the *thesis* part add? That comes from a Greek word meaning to "set," as to set in opposition. The other forms of the noun *antithesis*, of course, all involve the idea of opposites or opposition: the goals are in opposition, the means of achieving them are in opposition, and their slogans oppose each other.

A famous *antithesis* was used by President Jimmy
Carter in 1981: "America did not invent human
rights . . . human rights invented America."

The opposing ideas are exact opposites. *Antithesis* and its
plural, *antitheses*, are useful words to describe opposites in
many situations.

Now let's try another word beginning with an *a* and
having a negative idea: *abnegate*.

Although he *abnegated* his god, he would not
abnegate his power, and the people considered his
abnegation a betrayal of their trust in him.

You surely noticed the prefix *ab* and know it means
"from." You can speculate that *negate* must be related to
"negative," a word you probably use to say "no" to
something or cancel it.

To *abnegate* his god—that king must have denied his god
but not given up his throne. His people would, of course,
consider such inconsistency a betrayal if they had thought
him a god-believing leader.

Or it could have meant the president of a board who had
been put there by supporters of his good character, and they
felt betrayed when he gave up God but not his power as
president.

You're doing well as a word-meaning sleuth. *Abnegate*
does, indeed, mean to "deny" or "renounce" as well as to
"surrender" or "relinquish." And yes, it does share the
background of *negative*. *Self-abnegation*, of course, means
"self-denial," "renouncing oneself."

Let's look at another set of words.

> You might consider our discussion *discursive,* our *discursiveness* to be rambling rather than well directed.

That prefix *dis* usually means "not." You undoubtedly recognize the *cursive* part as being connected with "running" —as in *cursive* writing being running, as opposed to printing with the letters separated. However, a *cursory* glance is a quick one. So, *discursive* discussion must be the opposite of running or quick discussion—a discussion that is the result of analysis and reasoning. Right?

The answer again combines yes and no. That tracing of the pedigree is essentially correct, but the word has two rather distinct meanings. It can mean "rambling" from one thing to another, or it can mean "proceeding coherently" from one thing to another, marked by analytical reasoning.

How do you know which it means? By the context of the sentence. *Webster's* lists two first meanings: *a* is "rambling," and *b* is "proceeding coherently." That doesn't indicate a strong preference. So, examine the context carefully. Fortunately, *discursive* is often used with other adjectives and usually means "rambling."

> The speaker's *discursive* meander through his past experiences with the supernatural made staying awake a major challenge (obviously *discursive* means "rambling" here).

> The opposing team's *discursive* presentation of precise facts and succinct examples won the debate (just as obviously, here it means "proceeding coherently").

Let's try a complete change. *Banal* is an abused word. Until recently, it was pronounced as it had been in its original French, with the accent on the second syllable, the first *a* sounding like the *u* in "abut," and the second *a* sounding like the *a* in "ash": *banál*. We would say that *banál* (adjective) comments only added to the already overwhelming *banality* (noun) of the dull conversation.

Now, however, the accent often slips to the first syllable and the first *a* has lengthened to become *bā́nal*. With either pronunciation it means "trite" or "commonplace" as in boring and lacking originality. You may hear the accent on the first syllable as often as on the second.

Now for some R and R—recall and review. Meanings, please, of *literate* and *illiterate*. Answer mentally before reading the next paragraph.

> The adjective *literate* means "able to read and write" or "aware of good literature and other fine things" as in "cultured."
>
> *Illiterate* means "unable to read or write," "uneducated," or "unaware of correct behavior or terminology."

Next were *legible* and *illegible*.

> *Legible* means "readable" as in penmanship and *illegible* means "not readable" for the same reason.

And *readable* and *unreadable*?

> "Able to be read" and "not able to be read" because of poor penmanship, dullness, or inappropriateness.

How about *intelligible* and *unintelligible*?

"Capable of being comprehended" or "not capable of being comprehended."

Then there were those words *about* words. What is a *synonym*?

A word with the same meaning as another word.

And a *homonym*?

A word that sounds like another one but has a different meaning.

How about *antonym*?

That's a word with the opposite meaning from another.

Now trot through those next five. *Articulate?*

The adjective *articulate* means "clear" when you refer to speaking or expressing in words; "segmented" or "broken into portions" when you refer to enunciation or animals. The verb means to "speak."

Antithesis?

Antithesis means "opposite."

Abnegate?

Abnegate means to "deny" or "renounce."

There are just two left: *discursive* and *banal*.

Discursive usually means "rambling" but can mean "proceeding coherently."

Banal means "trite," "commonplace." The accent is moving to the first syllable—*bānal*.

Complete Exercises 1 and 2 and Pretest 2.

EXERCISE 1

Directions: Fill in each blank in the following sentences with the word that *best fits the meaning* of the sentence.

1. Even when educated Americans travel to Europe, they soon find that a foreign language makes them feel _____.

    discursive   banal   illiterate   articulate

2. Many colleges require their students to take public speaking, hoping that they will be _____ when facing audiences in the future.

    readable   literate   articulate   legible

3. The teacher asked Michael to label the words *plane* and *plain;* he correctly explained that they were _____.

    legible   unreadable   antonyms   homonyms

4. The teacher told the student that his paper on quasars would be _____ for most of the class.
  legible   unreadable   banal   articulate

5. Russian novelists seem to favor titles with _____ such as *War and Peace*.
  homonyms   legibility   articulateness
    antonyms

6. The _____ of capitalism is communism.
  abnegation   legibility   antithesis   illiteracy

7. To _____ smoking is to add years to your life, according to most doctors.
  articulate   abnegate   deprecate   disparage

8. Not only was the speaker's voice uninteresting, but most of his remarks seemed to be very ordinary or _____.
  legible   articulate   banal   literate

9. The crowd noise was so loud at the football game that remarks of the announcer were _____.
  banal   unintelligible   illegible   articulate

10. The ladies at the Thursday afternoon bridge session offer remarks that rarely pertain to bridge and become very _____.
  readable   articulate   discursive   legible

11. Fortunately, the journalist could type; his handwriting was never _____.
  discursive   legible   literate   intelligible

12. The snake model was called _____ because of the cleverly invisible way small sections were joined to provide lifelike movement.
  articulated   discursive   legible   deprecated

EXERCISE 2

Directions: On the lines in the following sentences, write the words in parentheses that *best fit the meanings* of the sentences.

1. In the citizenship classes, the teacher was not sure which of the new students were _____ (*literate, banal*).

2. _____ (*Illegible, Unintelligible*) writing can often be made readable by taking extra time.

3. The visiting professor used so many big words that his audience found his speech _____ (*illegible, unintelligible*).

4. John was sure of the meaning of synonyms, but he never felt easy about _____ (*homonyms, antonyms*), words that sound alike but have different meanings.

5. There is nothing as effective in ruining a stimulating conversation as _____ (a *banal*, an *articulate*) interruption.

6. Studying _____ (*antonyms, homonyms*) helps you discover words with opposite meanings.

7. Susan considered her brother's term paper very _____ (*readable, unreadable*) even though the topic did not hold her interest.

8. The immigrant stated that his arrival marked a complete _____ (*antithesis, abnegation*) of his former government.

9. The best antidote for _____ (*discursive, literate*) writing is a requirement that the writer discuss only one topic.

10. One of the best ways to test your points in an argument is to compare your position with the _____ (*antithesis, articulation*) of each statement.

11. In order to become more _____ (*articulate, literate*), the Greek orator Demosthenes is said to have practiced speaking with pebbles in his mouth.

12. She moved to an area of a major city noted for its _____ (*discursive, literate*) groups absorbed in assorted literary and artistic discoveries.

Pretest 2

Directions: Match the words in column A with the meanings in column B. On the line, write the word from column B that is *closest in meaning*.

A	B
1. diffident _____	disapprove
2. docile _____	physical pleasure
3. deprecate _____	repeating regularly
4. depreciate _____	degrade, discredit
5. disparage _____	at the same time
6. sensual _____	devalue, belittle
7. sensuous _____	continuing in sequence
8. continual _____	shy, reserved
9. continuous _____	without ceasing
10. continuity _____	following in sequence
11. concurrent _____	aesthetic enjoyment
12. consecutive _____	obedient, tractable

Section III, List 2

It will be beneficial to you to work on some more confusing pairs of words. With those you not only learn new words, you acquire some assurance that you won't use words that are similar but not correct. You get a serendipitous extra.

And away we go! Let's start with *diffident* and *docile*. Do you have any difficulty keeping those separated?

Diffident means "shy," "reserved." The connotation is that of being hesitant to act or speak because of a lack of self-confidence.

> Probably no one who felt *diffident* would be successful on the lecture circuit. The person's *diffidence* would prevent him or her from becoming active in politics, too.

You may think of *docile* people as being easy to lead. *Docility* seems to be the equivalent of obedience. Someone who is *docile*, obedient, could also be *diffident*, but the words really describe different characteristics. "Tractable" and "teachable" are also given as synonyms for *docile*.

Let's look at two more words beginning with *d: deprecate* and *depreciate*. These are unrelated but are often confused. To *deprecate* means to "disapprove of something and try to prevent it," as to *deprecate* all talk of war.

> Some might say that there were few things *deprecated*, deplored more in the United States than discrimination of any kind.

> A modest man may *deprecate* the idea that he's ahead of his time.

In the second example above, *deprecate* means to "gently disclaim credit" or to "politely contradict" someone. It's not a violent denial. This milder meaning is correct but less frequently used. The adjective *deprecatory* offers the same feeling—politely apologetic or wishing to avert something.

On the other hand, when the value of your house is *depreciated*, you need a stronger word. *Depreciate* means to "devalue," "lower the price." It's the opposite of *appreciate*, which means to "understand the value" of something or—in real estate—to "become more valuable."

When you speak of people, *depreciate* also means to "belittle," to "speak disparagingly or modestly" of something or someone.

The preferred use is to *deprecate* actions, to disapprove of them and try to avert them. Use *depreciate* when you mean to "show humility" toward people, including yourself as in *self-depreciating*.

Did you catch the word *disparage*? It's another word that has changed its meaning considerably as it developed from the Latin. It originally meant to "marry below one's class." It has come to mean to "degrade," to "*depreciate* indirectly," to "discredit," to "show disrespect for," to "speak slightingly of" as with *disparaging* remarks. It is often used as a synonym for *depreciate*, as we did.

Here's another pair long known to be troublemakers: *sensual* and *sensuous*. Probably one reason is that they are obviously from the same family—related to *sense*, *sensitive*, and *sensible*. The root word means feeling, sensation, perceiving. Both words can mean simply "related to the senses" or "gratifying the senses." Both have negative implications, too: self-indulgent, too fond of self-gratifying rewards, and the satisfaction of large appetites—especially in sex, food, or luxury.

They can also be used positively to indicate healthy satisfaction of senses. In reality, they are used interchangeably. Some experts recommend using *sensual* to refer to sexuality or other pleasures that gratify physical appetites, and *sensuous* for the more aesthetic pleasures. However, general usage makes that distinction less and less often. They're perfectly good words to use to refer to the satisfaction of senses, with the possible connotation of excessive interest in satisfying them.

Perhaps you are aware of many words that use the prefix *con,* meaning "with." You may also find several of them overlapping, difficult to separate. One pair is *continual* and *continuous*.

Join the experts. They differ noticeably. It would be a real challenge to compile all the opinions to determine the majority answer, so let's continue to use *Webster's* as our representative authority. There is a recognized distinction in meanings between *continual* and *continuous,* but that distinction is fading. However, appreciation remains with those who know the difference—and they judge those who don't observe it.

Both adjectives with their adverbs—*continual* and *continually, continuous* and *continuously*—mean "continuing through time." *Continual* and *continuous* rains are rains without pause.

Do they differ?

If you want to be absolutely correct, there are two areas where they differ in meaning.

> When you are referring to continuity through space, you use *continuous*: a *continuous* zone of warm air or a *continuous,* uninterrupted line of large trucks.

The other area is when you wish to refer to a regularly repeating occurrence. Then you should use the adjective *continual* or the adverb *continually: continual* waves on a beach—a repeating occurrence of waves.

Let's look at an example:

The rain in Spain fell *continually* on the plain; it stopped for five minutes each hour. Consequently, we hiked through a *continuous* flow of muddy water.

There's a closely related word we might mention: the noun *continuity* is used to refer to something that continues without interruption. The cast and events of soap operas, for example, provide *continuity* through many small plots. The person who writes scripts for such a series is called a *continuity* writer and may even provide a review of previous episodes to keep the plot development *continuous*, uninterrupted.

That could remind us of two more words beginning with *con* that confuse us. In newspaper accounts of trials and sentencing, we read about *concurrent* and *consecutive* sentences. Does *concurrent* mean what it means in other cases? Does the prefix *con* mean "with" and *current* mean "running together"?

That's it. *Concurrent* means "operating at the same time."

Concurrent resolutions are those that are passed by both houses of Congress at the same time.

Concurrent sentences run at the same time.

Concurrence is a coming together, an agreement.

To *concur* is to "act together" or to "express agreement."

Then *consecutive* must mean "following each other in sequence." So, *concurrent* sentences run at the same time, and *consecutive* sentences run one after the other. Can you imagine choosing *consecutive* sentences if you had a choice?

Please complete Exercises 3 and 4 and Pretest 3. Then we'll continue with a new group of prefixes.

EXERCISE 3

Directions: On the lines in the following paragraph, write the words in parentheses that *best fit the meanings* of the sentences.

There are many joys in having a home at the shore. Real estate values almost always rise rather than (1) _____ (*depreciate, deprecate*). Of course, bathing itself offers a (2) _____ (*sensual, sensuous*) pleasure, and there are the sunsets for (3) _____ (*sensual, sensuous*) enjoyment. Add to this the magic of waves in a (4) _____ (*continual, continuous*) procession marching to shore and the (5) _____ (*continual, continuous*) sea breeze filling the lungs with fresh, salt air. For the (6) _____ (*diffident, disparaging*) person afraid of the surf, walks on the beach and watching a flock of gulls land in a (7) _____ (*consecutive, concurrent*) manner are worthwhile. Although the surf rages during a northeaster, for the most part it remains a calm and (8) _____ (*docile, deprecated*) friend. Listen not to those who (9) _____ (*deprecate, depreciate*) a home at the shore. They are missing one of life's greatest joys. Their (10) _____ (*disparaging, diffident*) remarks usually indicate a lack of personal experience by the ocean. There is, however, the expense of maintaining two houses (11) _____ (*concurrently, continuously*), one in the city and one at the shore. Many are finding a solution in selling the family home and retiring to the shore to enjoy a (12) _____ (*continuity, concurrence*) of sea life all year long.

EXERCISE 4

Directions: Fill in each blank in the following sentences with the word that *best fits the meaning* of the sentence.

1. A person may be quiet and _____ at home but very boisterous when in a crowd.

    sensuous   vociferous   diffident   desultory

2. The brother seemed to _____ the efforts of his sister with negative remarks.

    depreciate   eulogize   praise   desultory

3. After a hard day's work, a good meal is one of life's _____ pleasures.

    sensual   sensuous   mundane   anomalous

4. In the winter, three different teams—football, basketball, and hockey—may have _____ schedules.

    continuous   concurrent   difficult
        exemplary

5. Usually a mortgage must be paid in _____ installments.

    contiguous   sensuous   consecutive   diffident

6. In an age of rebellion, to have a teenager who is on the _____ side is a blessing.

    sensual   docile   bovine   surly

7. He considered the _____ hammering next door an invasion of his privacy.

    banal   diffident   continual   concurrent

8. In the cold weather, the heat was kept on to offer _____ warmth.

   continuous   continuity   concurrent
   consecutive

9. The committee members _____ the efforts of the town council to push the new ruling into action without public reaction.

   praised   displayed   deprecated   encouraged

10. He was hired as a _____ writer to develop a weekly serial about black Americans.

    concurrent   continuous   continuity
    continual

11. The ballet master seemed to _____ all the efforts of the new dancer, upsetting her greatly.

    continue   disparage   docilize
    be diffident about

12. The entire opera filled him with an overwhelmingly _____ reaction to be long remembered.

    docile   sensual   sensuous   banal

Pretest 3

Directions: Match the words or prefixes in column A with the words in column B. On the line, write the word from column B that *is closest in meaning*.

A	B
1. uni– _____	believable, plausible
2. mono– _____	practicing self-denial, hermit
3. bi– _____	significant in history
4. tri– _____	highly combustible
5. quad– (quadra–, quadri)– ___	prefix meaning *one*
6. multi– _____	relating to history
7. credible _____	appreciating beauty
8. credulous _____	gullible, childlike
9. creditable _____	exciting, causing flames
10. historic _____	prefix meaning *two*
11. historical _____	bitingly severe, critical
12. acerbic _____	prefix meaning *many*
13. ascetic _____	prefix meaning *one*
14. aesthetic _____	prefix meaning *four*
15. flammable _____	worthy of praise or trust
16. nonflammable _____	prefix meaning *three*
17. inflammatory _____	not combustible

Section III, List 3

Now, what were those prefixes?

Let's play the numbers a bit. There are many prefixes that indicate a number as part of words, but we'll just discuss six now. What prefix indicates *one* of something?

> That's *uni*, as in *unicycle*—one wheel; *unicorn*—one horn; *uniform*—one form of clothing; and to bring together as one in *unify* and *unite*.

Another prefix meaning "one"? How about *mono*?

> *Monorail* is one rail, *monotone* is one tone, and a *monopoly* is controlled by one person or company.

Bi is a prefix meaning "two."

> A *bicycle* has two wheels, a *biped* has two feet, and to *bisect* is to cut or divide into two parts.

You're on the road to success!
Three is *tri*, of course, as in:

> *Tricycle, tricounty,* and *trio,* mean three wheels, three counties, and three people or things.

Next is *quad,* to indicate "four."

> A *quadrilateral* has four sides, a *quadruped* has four feet, and a *quadrangle* has four angles.

Notice the slight change in spelling: quadri in *quadrilateral*, quadru in *quadruped*, and quadra in *quadrangle*.

Rather than continue counting, consider a prefix that means many: *multi*. You are familiar with *multisensory*, "involving more than one sense"; *multilevel*, "having several levels"; and *multicopy*. In most dictionaries, you'll find lists of 150 or more words using this prefix.

Let's go back to eliminating confusion. Do you ever find that *credible*, *credulous*, and *creditable* are confusing?

> *Credible* means "believable." The manager gave me a *credible* reason for being late for our luncheon meeting, one I could believe.

> *Incredible* means "unbelievable," literally "not to be believed." That might describe the performance of a very clever magician: *Incredible!* Unbelievable!

> *Credulous* means "believing based on too little evidence." It's often associated with "childlike" —as *credulous* as a child.

We also have *credulity*, the noun meaning "lack of doubt or readiness to believe," and the adverb *credulously*, meaning "with belief." These words all come from the same root, of course: *credo* is Latin and means "I believe." The accent is on the *cred*, except in the noun when you accent *du, credúlity*.

The third one we mentioned—*creditable*—is not related. It has to do with credit. It means "worthy of credit, praise, or trust."

> You do a consistently *creditable* job of maintaining interest. You dig into confusing vocabulary most *creditably*.

Can you do the same for *historic* and *historical*? The distinction between them is worth remembering—and not difficult.

Historical is a good all-purpose adjective meaning "belonging to or concerned with history."

> You can have *historical* settings for books, documents in museums, costumes, or recipes. It merely refers to something in history, possibly connected with people or events we find in history books. Many old houses are designated *historical* because they represent an era, not because they are connected with any particular *historic* event.

An *historic* event is one that is considered significant in history, a specific part of history.

> We have the *historic* battle at Waterloo or winter at Valley Forge.

How about *acerbic*, *ascetic*, and *aesthetic*?

It helps to see those three to separate them. *Acerbic*, the adjective, and its friendly verb, *acerbate*, come from the Latin *acerbus*, meaning "sharp," "harsh," or "sour."

> *Acerbic* means "acid in temper, mood, or tone," "bitingly severe and critical."

> *Acerbic* wit is cruel, vicious.

> To *acerbate* means to "irritate and exasperate."

> Most of us work hard to avoid *acerbation* with a client or a friend; they don't appreciate cruelty.

Ascetic can be either a noun or an adjective. It refers to withdrawing rather than irritating.

> The noun indicates a hermit, an *ascetic,* one who practices strict self-denial for personal or religious reasons.

> The adjective describes the act of practicing or even the appearance or manner of self-denial. An *ascetic* may retreat to the desert and be seen occasionally attired in sackcloth and ashes as he *ascetically* meditates on *asceticism,* the belief that he can reach a higher spiritual state through self-denial.

That was impressive! And *aesthetic*? It refers to the principle or theory of beauty or satisfying one's perception of beauty.

> You may appreciate gemstones for their *aesthetic* value rather than their monetary worth.

> A Japanese feast may be an *aesthetic* experience. *Aesthetics* is a branch of philosophy dealing with beauty.

> You are an *aesthete*. You are highly sensitive to art and beauty. You may find an arrangement of winter roses to be totally overwhelming.

Aesthetes devote their energies to *aestheticism,* an appreciation of beauty. You sometimes see this word spelled without the initial *a*—just esthetic. That is a variation and is not more or less correct than with the *a*.

Those three have similar sounds unless they're very carefully pronounced, but their meanings don't approach one another at all.

We'd like to separate one more pair that really causes bewilderment. What's the difference between *flammable* and *inflammable*? Does that prefix *in* mean "in" or "not"?

Unless you've visited the firehouse recently, you may have to guess. You may also have trouble believing that they both mean "highly combustible," "able to be inflamed." The opposite term is *nonflammable*. *Inflammable* is the older term, but somewhere along the line, *flammable* came into use.

In many technical contexts, *flammable* is used to label highly combustible materials to avoid dangerous confusion.

Inflammable is used in other contexts, including in figurative senses—meaning "excitable," "easily angered," or "out of control." An *inflammable* temperament in an embassy may cause an *inflammable* state of international tension.

The only addition to that thorough picture is to add the adjective *inflammatory*, which means, obviously, "causing *inflammation*." It is used in the medical sense to mean "characterized by inflammation," in the fire-causing sense of causing a fire, and the figurative sense of exciting, arousing, or angering—as an *inflammatory* remark.

Now for a quick review. The prefixes that add specific numbers to words:

Uni and *mono* indicate "one," as in *unicycle* and *monotone*, one wheel and one tone.

Bi means "two" and *tri* means "three"—*bicycle* and *tricycle,* two or three wheels.

Quad is "four"—*quadrilateral,* four-sided.

Multi does not specify a number, but refers to more than one, as in *multisensory,* many senses.

Nice work! Now the confusing sets—those based on *credo.*

Credible means "believable."

Credulous means "believing."

Creditable, the third, is not based on *credo.* It means "worthy of credit."

The two words related to *history*?

Historic means "significant in history."

Historical refers to something that's just a part of history in general.

Then there are three *a*'s.

Acerbic means "nasty," "biting."

Ascetic means either a hermit or the behavior associated with one.

Aesthetic—sometimes spelled without the initial *a*—means "appreciating the beautiful things in life."

Our firehouse friends?

> *Flammable* means "easy to burn" and is the term used in technical contexts, with the opposite being *nonflammable*.

> *Inflammable* also means "easily ignited" and is stretched to mean "excitable," too.

> *Inflammatory* means "causing *inflammation*"—of tissue and muscle and temper.

Now it's time to complete Exercises 5 and 6 and Pretest 4.

EXERCISE 5

Directions: Fill in each blank in the following paragraph with the words in parentheses that *best fit the meanings* of the sentences.

Each year students are taken to the (1) _____ (*historical, historic*) firehouse, the oldest volunteer company in New Jersey and the forerunner of all others. On the walls are many (2) _____ (*historic, historical*) pictures of firemen with handlebar mustaches. One boy persisted in sharing an unhappy experience he'd had with a critical, (3) _____ (*acerbic, aesthetic*) neighbor who was a fireman. Observing the boy's (4) _____ (*flammable, inflammatory*) effect on the usually (5) _____ (*credible, credulous*) fourth-graders, the guide pointed out the (6) _____ (*aesthetic, ascetic*) qualities of the quaint building. His presentation was (7) _____ (*credulous, creditable*) and showed an understanding of his audience. Then he turned their attention to deciding which displayed materials were highly (8) _____ (*flammable, inflammatory*). The fireman explained that when they were on duty, they lived an (9) _____ (*ascetic, aesthetic*) existence; their job was to be ready and alert for a fire. A concluding story of personal experiences made the account (10) _____ (*inflammatory, credible*) for the entire group.

Directions: Fill in each blank in the following sentences with the appropriate prefix from the following group:

uni   mono   bi   tri   quad   quadru   multi

11. To mean many-layered, you can use the prefix _____layered.

12. We describe a four-legged creature as a _____ped.

13/14. _____ and _____ are prefixes meaning "one."

15. A meeting held every three years is a _____ennial.

16. A plane with two wings is a _____plane.

17. To multiply an amount by four is to _____ruple it.

EXERCISE 6

Directions: Fill in each blank in the following sentences with one of the following words:

acerbate	aesthetic	ascetic
credible	creditable	credulity
historic	historical	
inflammatory	nonflammable	

1. When it comes to discussing things related to history, _____ refers to items typical of various periods.
2. _____ refers to items connected with specific events in history.
3. In an effort to avoid confusion, _____ is recommended as the adjective to use for material not highly combustible.
4. An _____ remark may cause irritation or a fiery reaction.
5. Controlling angry, depreciating remarks is _____ and usually brings you favorable recognition.
6. The _____ of children is to be respected, not undermined by deceit.
7. A statement that can be believed is _____.
8. To _____ is to hurt others with criticism or sarcasm.
9. Relatively few people take the time to withdraw for the purely _____ experience of meditation.
10. An _____ delight in fine art gives great sensuous satisfaction.

Pretest 4

Directions: Match the meanings in column A with the words in column B. On the line, write the word from column B that *is closest in meaning*.

A		B
1. keep small _____		activate
2. make certain _____		activism
3. to begin, start _____		initiate
4. one who organizes, manages _____		enterprise
5. put into action _____		entrepreneur
6. project or undertaking _____		ascertain
7. taking action on controversial issue ____		minimize
8. make the most of _____		maximize

Section III, List 4

Corporate consultants spend much time emphasizing the importance of using *action* words in speaking and writing— even on a resumé. How about looking at a few of them?

As a beginning, what does *activate* mean?

Did you say, "Put into action"? Right . . . but how? Think about the uses of that word.

> You can *activate* a bomb by releasing something that keeps it from going off.

> You can *activate* a machine by connecting it to a source of power.

Then there's *activating* nuclear power with radio-
active molecules.

You also *activate* plans by putting them into
operation.

Notice that you have mentioned two different activities:
providing what was needed to make something act, or
removing whatever kept it from acting. It can include
organizing or setting up a group of people as in *activating* a
military unit. We even use it to *activate* sewage—to mix it
with air in order to encourage the growth of organisms that
cause decomposition. So let's look at some words to get you
moving, to get you into action.

One we read in newspapers is *activism*. How is that
related to action?

You might say that's a policy of taking very direct action
and think of it in connection with demonstrations in favor
of or against political causes.

That is the way we most often hear it. *Activism* involves
taking action after making a decision about some controversial issue.

What about *initiative*? Is that related?

You can see that that must be related to *initial*, and
your initials are the first letters of your names. So, *initiative*
must be the act of beginning something. But the emphasis is
on causing something to start.

If you *initiate* an idea or a program, you set it into
motion, you use *initiative*. If you're writing a
resumé, that's worth mentioning.

If you provided the *initiative*, if you had a good
idea and were the first to *activate* a money-saving
procedure, you showed *enterprise*.

You should also mention how *enterprising* you are
in your resumé.

Could you speculate what *enterprise* meant from that
context? *Enterprising* has the denotation of being marked by
an energetic, independent spirit and by a readiness to
undertake or experiment. In fact, the noun *enterprise* indicates a project or undertaking that is especially difficult,
complicated, or risky.

Another term for an *enterpriser* is *entrepreneur*. You
certainly hear that often these days! An *entrepreneur* is
usually a business owner.

The word comes from a root meaning to "undertake."
The usual meaning is "one who organizes, manages, and
assumes the risks of a business or enterprise." However,
you can display *entrepreneurial* ability even when you
manage someone else's business. And such ability is always
of value to other managers.

Those two words beginning with *e* would be good ones to
mention in a resumé—as long as they're true.

Before you brag, you'd better *ascertain* if you
really qualify—if you really do show *enterprise*
and *entrepreneurship*—or your prospective employer may *ascertain* that you have more ability
to stretch the truth than you have *initiative*.

From those sentences, you undoubtedly were able to
guess that *ascertain* means to "make certain," to "find
out" or "learn with certainty." You can see the word
certain in it.

The noun is *ascertainment,* and the adjective is
ascertainable. Unlike *certain*, the accent is on
tain in all three words.

One other thing you should do in a resumé is to *minimize* your shortcomings and *maximize* your good qualities. Those are good short-cut words—words that can save your using several words. The meanings are obvious:

> Keep to a *minimum;* discuss a *minimum* amount, as little as possible.

> Expand to the *maximum;* make the most of, the greatest amount possible.

> Make the *maximal* impression with your unlimited accomplishments and potential.

Serendipity: in this country, *maximize* ends in *ize;* in Britain, it's *ise*.

Minimize and *minimal* are used in rather special ways, too. *Minimal art* and *minimalism* refer to art using the fewest and simplest elements for the greatest effect—often geometric shapes. A *minimalist* believes in restricting to a *minimum* the functions and powers of a political organization.

For a review, consider how these eight words will help you sell yourself to a prospective employer:

> You'll *maximize* your strengths, your ability to *activate* sleepy salespeople, your ability to take the *initiative* as a valuable and *enterprising entrepreneur* who is gifted in *ascertaining* high-profit items. But you had better *minimize* your *activism* in certain areas that might be misinterpreted.

With that package of review, it's time to complete Exercises 7 and 8 and Pretest 5. Then we'll look at another small group of words that causes us problems in knowing exactly what is meant.

EXERCISE 7

Directions: On the lines in the following sentences, write the words in parentheses that *best fit the meanings* of the sentences.

1. There was much concern over the decision to _____ (*activate, ascertain*) the nuclear plant at Three Mile Island.
2. In many areas, objection to the building of nuclear power plants has led to community _____ (*etymology, activism*).
3. If we could _____ (*initiate, ascertain*) the cause of the common cold, many people would shout for joy.
4. In our era, the flight to the moon was an _____ (*enterprise, compendium*) Americans viewed with great pride.
5. When a person runs one restaurant he's called a manager; if he expands it to a chain, he's _____ (an *entrepreneur,* a *broker*).
6. His friends were amazed when he finally displayed the _____ (*initiative, activation*) to establish a successful design studio.
7. If you _____ (*enterprise, minimize*) your overhead, your business will probably make a profit.
8. Instead of driving, walk or bike on many small errands to _____ (*maximize, ascertain*) your circulation.

EXERCISE 8

Directions: On the lines in the following paragraph write the words in parentheses that *best fit the meanings* of the sentences.

During the sixties, (1) _____ (*activism, enterprise*) was rampant on college campuses. A number of students sought to (2) _____ (*activate, minimize*) some type of plan for their own particular groups. To (3) _____ (*minimize, ascertain*) their impact, police often had to be called to restore order. The college deans had trouble (4) _____ (*predicting, ascertaining*) just which group on campus was responsible for (5) _____ (*enterprising, initiating*) demonstrations. Sadly, if the college administrators were there to (6) _____ (*disparage, maximize*) a student's academic ability during this period, that aim was thwarted. However, some studies have indicated that personal ability to organize any (7) _____ (*enterprise, minimum*) and manage its development resulted in later (8) _____ (*entrepreneurs, researchers*) from among the groups of students who learned to focus on an idea, arrange financial support, and delegate responsibilities.

Pretest 5

Directions: Match the words in column A with the meanings in column B. On the line, write the word from column B that is *closest in meaning*.

	A		B
1.	regardless	_____	morally correct
2.	importune	_____	suitable, convenient
3.	opportune (adj)	_____	correct judgment
4.	rectitude	_____	urge persistently (verb)
			overly persistent (adj)
5.	righteous	_____	in spite of

Section III, List 5

This program is somewhat like cleaning house; we're about to tackle another closet of long-avoided, consistently ignored words that we can't use because we're not 100 percent sure of their meanings. In cleaning out the unused and nonessential, we often discover forgotten treasures!

You often see *regardless* and *irregardless* used interchangeably. Are they as confused in use as *flammable* and *inflammable*?

The answer depends on whether you refer to a dictionary or a book of correct English usage. The dictionary will say that *irregardless* is a nonstandard or humorous word used in place of *regardless*. A book guiding you to correct usage will list *irregardless* as a nonword. Some even state that there is no such word.

Dictionaries record usage, and the word is obviously used. Experts on usage consider *irregardless* totally incorrect, but their label of "nonword" is wishful thinking. We've heard the word. However, there is no such word in acceptable English. The word is *regardless* and means "in spite of," "without taking into account."

> Parents and children should try for common grounds *regardless* of the generation gap—in spite of it, without considering it.

So, we had a nonword!

Both of these exist: *importune* and *opportune*. Do you know what each means? They sound and look much alike, but they have very different meanings.

Importune can be either a verb meaning to "urge with troublesome persistence" or an adjective meaning "overly persistent." It's often associated with butting in, interrupting to demand attention.

> A friend who acts *importunely*, who is an *importuner*, is a nuisance and soon loses all friends because of his *importunity*, his constant nagging and demanding.

So, to *importune* means to "annoy with demands," to "beg urgently." And *opportune*? You might speculate that it is related to *opportunity*. It is. It's an adjective that means "at a suitable or convenient or appropriate time."

> An *opportune* moment is one that offers an *opportunity* for goal accomplishment.

Offering assistance at an *opportune* time means you might be rewarded for the appropriateness of your offer.

You are an *opportunist* when you select the appropriate time to seize your *opportunity* to mention that you're an *enterprising entrepreneur*.

There is no verb form, but there are three nouns and two adjectives:

Opportunity means "favorable circumstances"; *opportunism* means the "policy or practice of taking advantage of *opportunities*"; and an *opportunist* is the person using the *opportunities* available.

An *opportune* event is one that offers an *opportunity*, and if you are *opportunistic*, you do grasp *opportunities*.

We have two more. They must have to do with *right* because they sound like they should: *righteousness* and *rectitude*. One has the word *right* in it, and the other must be a form of the verb to *rectify*, which means to "make right."

Good logic. In fact, they are given as synonyms in some dictionaries. In many cases they can be used interchangeably, but there are slightly different connotations.

Although they both mean "uprightness," *righteousness* connotes "right" according to morality, morally justifiable.

A *righteous* decision is one based on moral values.

That *righteous indignation* you hear about is indignation based on strong moral belief. It can be a

bit stuffy—an outraged sense of justice with accompanying judgment of what is just. It sometimes also includes patting yourself on the back—
being *self-righteous*.

Rectitude means the "state of being correct in judgment
or procedure," "being error-free." The synonym is *correct*
rather than "moral." *Rectification* means "correction" or
"adjustment to correct." It can refer to the time on a clock
as well as a moral decision.

It's time now to complete Exercises 9 and 10. Before you
go any further, however, nail down any uncertainties or
confusions, and go over any words you find especially
difficult until you feel you're in command. A good review
pays dividends.

EXERCISE 9

Directions: On the lines in the following paragraph, write
   the words in parentheses that *best fit the meanings* of the
   sentences.

Although it was the (1) _____ (*importune, opportune*)
moment to ask for a raise, Jason had (2) _____ (*importuned, disparaged*) with such insistence that his request was
denied. This puzzled him; his work had been a model of
(3) _____ (*righteousness, rectitude*), of correct judgment. Even his outside activities, concern with church and
neighborhood development, had been marked by (4)
_____ (*rectitude, righteousness*), moral correctness.
Bitter, he decided that (5) _____ (*regardless, irregardless*) of one's record, there was nothing guaranteed when
one works for someone else.

EXERCISE 10

Directions: On the lines in the following sentences, write the words in parentheses that *best fit the meanings* of the sentences.

1. The son said he was going to take the family car _____ (*irregardless, regardless*) of the consequences.

2. If you _____ (*importune, ascertain*) your friend for favors every moment of the day, you will lose that friend.

3. Some people never seem to know when the _____ (*articulate, opportune*) moment presents itself for a request.

4. There are those who question the president on his _____ (*rectitude, righteousness*) in making wise political decisions.

5. Many feel that the pope has been traveling too much, but no one seems to doubt his _____ (*corpulence, righteousness*).

Pretest 1

1. homonyms
2. unintelligible
3. articulate
4. literate
5. antithesis
6. illiterate
7. legible
8. discursive
9. antonyms
10. banal
11. unreadable
12. abnegate
13. readable

Exercise 1

1. illiterate
2. articulate
3. homonyms
4. unreadable
5. antonyms
6. antithesis
7. abnegate
8. banal
9. unintelligible
10. discursive
11. legible
12. articulated

Exercise 2

1. literate
2. illegible
3. unintelligible
4. homonyms
5. a banal
6. antonyms
7. readable
8. abnegation
9. discursive
10. antithesis
11. articulate
12. literate

Pretest 2

1. shy, reserved
2. obedient, tractable
3. disapprove
4. devalue, belittle
5. degrade, discredit
6. physical pleasure
7. aesthetic enjoyment
8. repeating regularly
9. without ceasing
10. continuing in sequence
11. at the same time
12. following in sequence

Exercise 3

1. depreciate
2. sensual
3. sensuous
4. continual
5. continuous
6. diffident
7. consecutive
8. docile
9. deprecate
10. disparaging
11. concurrently
12. continuity

Exercise 4

1. diffident
2. depreciate
3. sensual
4. concurrent
5. consecutive
6. docile
7. continual
8. continuous
9. deprecate
10. continuity
11. disparage
12. sensuous

Pretest 3

1. prefix meaning *one*
2. prefix meaning *one*
3. prefix meaning *two*
4. prefix meaning *three*
5. prefix meaning *four*
6. prefix meaning *many*
7. believable, plausible
8. gullible, childlike
9. worthy of praise or trust
10. significant in history
11. relating to history
12. bitingly severe, critical
13. practicing self-denial, hermit
14. appreciates beauty
15. highly combustible
16. not combustible
17. exciting, causing flames

Exercise 5

1. historic
2. historical
3. acerbic
4. inflammatory
5. credulous
6. aesthetic
7. creditable
8. flammable
9. ascetic
10. credible
11. multi
12. quadru
13. uni
14. mono
15. tri
16. bi
17. quad

Exercise 6

1. historical
2. historic
3. nonflammable
4. inflammatory
5. creditable
6. credulity
7. credible
8. acerbate
9. ascetic
10. aesthetic

Pretest 4

1. minimize
2. ascertain
3. initiate
4. entrepreneur
5. activate
6. enterprise
7. activism
8. maximize

Exercise 7

1. activate
2. activism
3. ascertain
4. enterprise
5. an entrepreneur
6. initiative
7. minimize
8. maximize

Exercise 8

1. activism
2. activate
3. minimize
4. ascertaining
5. initiating
6. maximize
7. enterprise
8. entrepreneurs

Pretest 5

1. in spite of
2. urge persistently
3. suitable, convenient
4. correct judgment
5. morally correct

Exercise 9

1. opportune
2. importuned
3. rectitude
4. righteousness
5. regardless

Exercise 10

1. regardless
2. importune
3. opportune
4. rectitude
5. righteousness

SECTION IV

Please complete Pretest 1, below, for Section IV before we go any further. (See p. 196 for the correct answers to the tests and exercises in this section.)

Pretest 1

Directions: Match the words in column A with the meanings in column B. On the line, write the word from column B that is *closest in meaning*.

A	B
1. idiolect _____	slang or specialized vocabulary
2. dialect _____	legal document
3. colloquialism _____	denounce, remove skin
4. jargon _____	individual speech pattern
5. venue _____	location
6. beneficiary _____	addition to a will
7. brief (noun) _____	agent of change
8. codicil _____	regional speech pattern
9. catalyst _____	gift recipient
10. exacerbate _____	treelike
11. excoriate _____	conversational expression
12. stellar (adj) _____	outstanding
13. arboreal _____	aggravate, make worse

151

SECTION IV, LIST 1

You may have heard that each of us has his or her own *idiolect*. You may have speculated from the context that that meant your speech pattern is unlike anyone else's—is as unique as your fingerprints. But do you notice that much difference in the speech patterns you hear from others?

Probably not. Our ears aren't attuned to the minute differences in speech patterns—including pronunciation, intonation, word choice, grammar, inflection, method of emphasizing words, pauses, and everything else that goes into our individual style of speech. That's what *idiolect* means: the speech pattern of an individual.

Idiolect is related to *dialect*. All the *idiolects* of an area or a social group share a common core of language features—of New York City or Boston or Harvard graduates—and are grouped together to form a *dialect*. Every *dialect* has a set of common features that distinguish it from other *dialects*.

When the common tie is geographical, we call it a *regional dialect;* when it is a social grouping, we call it a *social dialect*. In the United States, for example, we have a New England *dialect*, a southern *dialect*, and a western *dialect*.

Dialects are usually understood as long as the distance between the two groups of people is not too great; they aren't really separate languages. A language is a continuous chain of dialects, of regional variations of the language.

We talked of *vernacular* when we discussed malapropisms. We said that meant the everyday speech of an area, usually the speech of the common man as opposed to the well-educated setter of standards. There are two more words about speech: *colloquialism* and *jargon*. A *colloquialism* is a word or expression used in conversation. *Colloquial* speech is characterized by words and phrases of informal speech. The label *colloquial* is listed in most dictionaries as "conversational and informal," not necessarily substandard or incorrect.

A *colloquy* is a conversation, especially an informal one. Closely associated with *colloquial* is *slang*. That refers to words that are in common use but whose meanings are adapted by a special group. High school students, for example, have their own *slang* vocabulary. In *slang*, common words have special meanings:

> *Dough* and *bread* and *lettuce* have long meant "money."
>
> *Skirt, broad,* and many other denote "girl."
>
> *Jock* means an "athletic type of man."

Slang stands between the acceptable general vocabulary and the in-group words that are called *jargon*. The first meaning given for *jargon* is "incoherent, meaningless talk." The second meaning is "simplified vocabulary for communication between peoples of different speech." In common use now, *jargon* refers to the terminology of a special group—the specialized vocabularies by which members of particular groups communicate among themselves. It may include technical terms understood by members of the group but not outsiders in general. It may be a form of elitism, a conscious exclusion of those not in the group. Even when the choice of words is necessary—as in legal *jargon*—it is often made unnecessarily obscure and obfuscating.

> When a lawyer persists in saying "change of *venue*" instead of "change of location" when he speaks with laymen, you may wonder about his motive.

On the other hand, many terms formerly used only by the legal profession have become common in the conversation of laymen:

> *Beneficiary* refers to someone who benefits from a will or legacy or an insurance policy, but it can also refer to someone who benefits from nonlegal consideration—when you act with special kindness, you may have no specific *beneficiary* in mind. Anyone who benefits may be the beneficiary of my *beneficence*, my kindness.

> In law, a *brief* is a document prepared by an attorney to provide an overview of the client's case. The verb *brief* means to "give precise instructions" to a witness about what to say in a trial.

> We also *brief* business partners before conferences and astronauts before takeoff. In this sense, it means to "coach them thoroughly." *Debriefing* them after they return means "learning from them."

> *Codicil* is used to mean an "appendix," a "supplement," "something added." In legal *jargon*, it usually refers to something added to a will after the original writing.

The recent trend has been to try to make legal documents more readable by laypeople, but the person needing to read such documents should become aware of the meanings of the most frequently used terms. There are legal dictionaries, but all dictionaries give brief meanings.

The same is true with other specialized jargon, of course. We use several terms from scientific jargon in our general vocabularies. What is a *catalyst*?

In chemistry, a *catalyst* is an agent or substance that causes a chemical reaction without itself being changed. A *catalyst* initiates a chemical reaction. In nonscientific use, it refers to someone or something that causes a significant change. History is full of books that acted as *catalysts* for revolutions, that had catalytic influences on decisions to revolt.

Are you familiar with the word *excoriate*? Its common meaning is to "condemn" or "denounce." You read of a senator *excoriating* welfare frauds.

> The first meaning of *excoriate* in most dictionaries is to "wear off or strip off the skin." The etymology goes back to the Latin word for skin—*corium*. Add the prefix *ex* and you have the idea. An *excoriation* is an abrasion.

Sometimes confused with *excoriate* is *exacerbate*. How about a speculation about its meaning.

Yes, *exacerbate* looks a lot like *acerbic*. As you remember, that means "acid," and "irritating." *Exacerbate* means to "make more harsh or bitter," to "make a situation worse."

> Some drugs *exacerbate* heart problems; they aggravate them.

So, *excoriate* means to "remove skin" or to "denounce," and *exacerbate* means to "make a situation worse," medical or otherwise. *Stellar* is another word we borrow from the world of science. It refers, of course, to the stars or to being made up of stars. Our nonscientific use of it is based on the use of "star" to describe a leading performer in the theater or on the concert stage, or even sports or classes of advertised products.

We have Broadway stars who are given *stellar* billing for *stellar* performances and have reputations of being *stellar* attractions.

You often see them on TV reminding you that the red sportscars they own are of *stellar* quality.

The woman's name Stella is from the same source.

What about the word *arboreal*? *Arboreal* animals live in trees, and an *arboretum* is a place where trees and plants are cultivated for scientific study. But we also have *arboretums* where people go for enjoyment of the beauty rather than scientific examination of varieties.

Perhaps your grandmother had an *arbor* that was a kind of trellis covered with grape vines.

An *arborist* specializes in the care and maintenance of trees.

Then there's *Arbor* Day, when many communities plant trees.

Let's have a quick review of the thirteen words so far in this section.

Idiolect: Individual speech pattern.

Dialect: Speech patterns common to one area or social class.

Colloquialism: Words or phrases for informal conversation.

Jargon: The vocabulary used by a particular group, often by one profession.

Venue, in legal jargon: Location; often where events causing legal action take place, or the place from which a jury is drawn or where it sits. (Added information is a serendipity!)

Beneficiary: One who benefits—either through legal designation or just through enjoying benefits of someone's kindness.

Brief: An overview of a legal case or a set of instructions to inform a person or a group, particularly legal clients, business associates, astronauts, members of the press, or others needing precise details.

Codicil: An addition to a will or a supplement to a monthly report.

Now the five from scientific roots:

Catalyst: The agent causing an action or reaction, the initiator of action.

Excoriate: To skin or to condemn—or both.

Exacerbate: To irritate or aggravate a medical or any other kind of situation.

Stellar: Relating to stars—in the sky or in the theater.

Arboreal: Relating to trees.

Let's put it in writing by completing Exercises 1 and 2 and Pretest 2.

EXERCISE 1

Directions: On the lines in the following paragraph, write the words in parentheses that *best fit the meanings* of the sentences.

Mildred had a fear of lawyers, mainly because she thought they spoke in a (1) _____ (*jargon, venue*) foreign to her. Not that her own lawyer's (2) _____ (*dialect, codicil*) was very different from hers, since they had grown up in the same area. She went to see him about her father's will. She had been named (3) _____ (*beneficiary, codicil*). A younger sister had not been included in the will and was seeking, through another lawyer, a (4) _____ (*venue, codicil*) to the will. Mildred was (5) _____ (*exacerbated, inundated*) by this action. Right in front of her lawyer, she began to (6) _____ (*eulogize, excoriate*) her sister. He calmed her down with a few (7) _____ (*colloquialisms, catalysts*), assuring her she had been a (8) _____ (*stellar, aboreal*) daughter. Furthermore, he stated the younger sister's (9) _____ (*brief, venue*) would not stand up in court. Mainly it was a (10) _____ (*catalyst, dialect*) for upsetting the family. He also said Mildred could request a change of location for the hearing, a change of (11) _____ (*brief, venue*). The whole problem engulfed Mildred, appearing (12) _____ (*arboreal, stellar*) with its many overpowering branches.

EXERCISE 2

Directions: On the following lines, write the words that *best fit the meanings*.

1. idiolect _____
    speech pattern of a group   jargon   venue
        individual speech pattern

2. colloquialism _____
    venue   speech impediment
        conversational expression   idiolect

3. venue _____
    catalyst   location   slang   treelike

4. beneficiary _____
    codicil   brief   gift recipient   arboreal

5. codicil _____
    individual speech   jargon   addition to a will
        venue

6. catalyst _____
    agent of change   regional expression
        speech pattern   slang

7. exacerbate _____
    stand out   soothe   aggravate, make worse
        express

8. dialect _____
    venue   individual speech pattern
        regional speech pattern   brief

9. brief (noun) _____
    venue   legal document   gift   change

10. excoriate _____
　　extoll　　denounce　　venerate　　implicate

11. stellar _____
　　outstanding　　overpowering　　sensual
　　sensuous

12. arboreal _____
　　starry　　flimsy　　of a tree　　of the stars

13. jargon _____
　　legal document　　brief　　specialized vocabulary
　　codicil

Pretest 2

Directions: Match the words in column A with the meanings in column B. On the line, write the word from column B that is *closest in meaning*.

A	B
1. interface _____	nonmetallic element used in compounds
2. debug _____	result
3. input _____	organic compound used for lubricants
4. throughput _____	remove errors
5. output _____	as desired, freely
6. silicon _____	make up on the spot
7. silicone _____	information entered, comment
8. ad lib _____	without notes
9. improvise _____	productivity
10. extemporaneous _____	plot outline
11. scenario _____	work together, communicate
12. protagonist _____	imitation of style
13. parody _____	leading character

Section IV, List 2

Let's get back to borrowing from the professions. The most obvious one recently has been the invasion from the computer industry. You may be getting a little tired of *interfacing, inputting, throughputting,* and *outputting.* Do you suppose that's because it's all so new and exciting? Some of those terms are approaching the cliché class. They are used too frequently to maintain fresh-sounding communication, and they are losing much of their meaning. Perhaps a little mental picture will help you realize that there are other words to serve the same purposes.

Visualize a computer terminal on your desk, receiving anything you choose to feed it. In spite of the mistakes attributed to them, computers print out only what has been put into them. The data going through them is put out without any addition—no intelligent reaction whatsoever. The facts can, of course, be rearranged and regrouped.

However, in most situations requiring communication between people, we provide information to other people to receive intelligent evaluations or to prompt intelligent reactions. Robot action is not usually commendable in a participating member of society. When we use *input* instead of more human verbs like "discuss," "state," "plead," or "inform," we dehumanize our contribution. Be sure that's what you want to do. There are better words to say what you want to say in most cases.

By the way, *input* isn't a recent word. The noun *input* was first added to official vocabulary lists in 1753. It meant the "amount put in"—the input of fertilizer increased crop yield. It was not used as a verb meaning to "enter data into a computer" until 1946.

Throughput is defined as "productivity based on the time it takes to input, process, and output information on a computer system." It isn't just the process of moving through.

Output, first defined in 1858 as "something produced," can include minerals mined or artistic and literary production.

> Currently, the most common application is to information fed out by a computer or an accounting machine. It can also be a verb: to *output* means to "produce."

Interface is really the point or means of interacting between data-processing systems or parts of a single system. We use it in the sense of working together, communicating.

No one knows what these terms will mean ten years from now, when they are further adapted to various uses.

Then there's *debug*. It, too, comes from computer jargon. In that field, it means to "find and remove errors from the design or the operation of a program."

> You hear it used to denote getting rid of anything that's not exactly right. The mechanic says he'll *debug* your car when you take it in for service. It can also mean to "remove hidden microphones or wiretapping devices." Incidentally, *debug* didn't enter the list of recorded words until 1950.

Another one is *bottom line*. It long ago lost its connection with accounting—on the computer or otherwise—and is used by sportswriters, salespersons, and schoolteachers. It originally meant, of course, the accountant's final figure on a balance sheet.

Now it's used to mean "final analysis," "inescapable result," or "complete summary." In many instances, it may provide a precise idea of finality, but its overuse has put it in the cliché class of vague meaning.

We have *bottom lines* of partnerships, political victories, or medical diagnoses.

Most dictionaries still define it as "concerned only with costs or profits, the net profit per share of stock."

"Most important consideration or ultimate decision" are listed as meanings when the term is used as slang.

Bottom line, like most clichés, is better avoided if you want your writing and speaking to sound more intelligent.

Another pair of words related to the computer industry that many find confusing is *silicone* and *silicon*. *Silicon* Valley is frequently mentioned in newscasts. Surely, that's not a valley made of *silicon*.

Nontechnical people often confuse the two terms.

Silicon is a hard, nonmetallic element that is used as, among other things, a semiconductor in transistors and computer chips.

That's the reason why the heartland of the microelectronics industry in Santa Clara and San Mateo counties in California is called Silicon Valley.

Silicone is an organic compound of silicon and oxygen. Its many uses include lubricants and artificial limbs.

You can associate *silicon* with microelectronics and *silicone* with oils and plastics. You won't be given any awards for a scientific approach, but that comparison may be helpful for the nonscientific—very nonscientific.

Still on the subject of translating terms from specific to general use, we lift several terms from the context of the theater for use in other areas. It follows a pattern when so much of our language comes from Greek and Latin roots, and our theater is built on the same foundation. Many people don't realize they're using theatrical terms even when they use the Latin.

> *Ad lib* can be used as a noun, an adjective, or an adverb. The date provided for the earliest recorded use varies, but 1610 is given for the longer version, *ad libitum*. It was an adverb meaning "in accordance with desire." The example was, "The rats fed *ad libitum*."

> By 1769 it was listed as an adverb meaning "omissible according to the performer's wishes."

> By 1919 the verb to *ad lib* meant "deliver spontaneously," to "improvise"—especially the lines of a play or a speech.

> Now, of course, we use the words to describe any message spoken without preparation. To be called upon to *ad lib* can be embarrassing when you haven't organized your thoughts beforehand.

A similar term is *improvise*. A frequent speaker might say:

> As a matter of fact, I'm pretty good at *improvisation*. My *improvisational* ability is limited only by

my audience. On almost any occasion I'm a great *improvisor*.

You may have trouble creating interesting thoughts *extemporaneously*, thinking them up on the spot without previous planning—without a script. You may not *extemporize* well.

Improvise and *extemporize* are synonyms that mean "make up on the spot." They can also refer to making use of what is available in a makeshift manner.

> When you lack an ingredient called for in a recipe, you *improvise*.

> Words spoken without much previous thought may be described as *extemporaneous*.

> *Extemporaneous* speeches may be well planned but delivered without notes, without any visible memory aids.

> Most beginning actors are given situations to act out *extemporaneously* to show their ability to *improvise*.

Another word from a theatrical background is *scenario*. It moved from meaning a "plot outline" used by actors, to the libretto of an opera, to the script for shooting a movie, to any sequence of events, especially when imagined and projected into the future.

Many creative people write a mental script of how some project should develop. The frustrating part is that not everyone else working on the project sees the same *scenario*. In fact, they often have to revise the *scenario* to oblige a *protagonist*.

Originally, in Greek tragedy, the *protagonist* was the leading character on whom the play centered. You now hear it as it was used in the paragraph above: the leader of a cause, a champion.

> The *protagonists* at a meeting may be the two main rivals attempting to win their respective points. Even when it is limited to one person, the noun sometimes means a "supporter of an idea or a cause"—perhaps because of the prefix *pro*.
>
> Acceptable meanings include both "a single leading character, often struggling against his destiny," or "two main characters in a power struggle."
>
> Woody Allen said of his problems, "I brought it on myself like the tragic *protagonist* of a Greek play." What a dramatic way to say, "I can't blame anyone else!"

Woody is also very good at *parodies*. But he creates parodies only for light humor, not ridicule. Some insensitive people criticize through *parodies*, through imitations.

Now can you *parody* a complete command of the last thirteen words?

First there were five associated with computerese:

> *Interface* means to "connect data-processing systems," and we use it to mean the "ability to face each other and cooperate."
>
> *Input, throughput,* and *output* refer to communication with the computer's central processing unit and the productivity related to the time involved, but we use them without reference to computers.

To *input* means to "inform," the *throughput* is
the rate of productivity or the amount of material
put through a process in a given period, and the
output is the product itself.

That's a summary, a simplification of those ideas, but it
may help you remember them. A purist may want to *debug*
such oversimplification, eliminate it.
Now the element and compound.

Silicon is a hard, nonmetallic element used as a
semiconductor in transistors and computer chips.
Silicon Valley is an area overflowing with micro-
electronic companies.

Silicone is an organic compound used in lubricants and artificial limbs.

You're right; you do know those. They must have been of
interest to you. We agreed earlier that interest is a vital
ingredient of learning.
How about the six related to the theater?

Perhaps you'd rather not *ad lib* or *improvise*,
rather not speak without previous thought.

You can use what's available to develop substi-
tutes for what's needed in recipes, however; you
can *improvise*.

You probably don't mind *extemporaneous* speaking when you can plan what you're going to say,
then put your notes aside.

You plan the *scenario* and visualize the smiling faces you'll see in front of you.

Your *scenario* probably sees you as the only *protagonist* with no other competing *protagonist*—to use the two meanings of the word, "main actor" or "competitor."

You may want to write a *parody,* an imitation, of a talking dictionary—just for gentle fun, not for ridicule.

Now let's take time for written review. Please complete Exercises 3 and 4 and Pretest 3 before we try to untangle some more meanings.

EXERCISE 3

Directions: On the lines in the following paragraph, write
the words in parentheses that *best fit the meanings* of the
sentences.

A new era in technology brings new terminology. One
striking term is (1) _____ (*Silicon, Silicone*) Valley,
referring to the area in California where much of the
computer industry is located. A compound with a similar-
sounding name, (2) _____ (*silicone, silicon*), is used
in prostheses. In California many scientists are (3)
_____ (*interfacing, excavating*) over new computer
models. Some are there to (4) _____ (*debug, parody*)
developing products, while others are concerned with how
much (5) _____ (*input, enterprise*) a computer can
hold. Still others, office managers, are concerned about the
(6) _____ (*throughput, debug*), the total efficiency of
production. Even though America has been leading in the
production of microchips, one (7) _____ (*scenario,
ad lib*) puts the Japanese as a major force, soon to become
the (8) _____ (*protagonist, impostor*) of the microchip
industry. Today, computer games (9) _____ (*parody,
debug*) real battles, as a generation ago youngsters arranged
mock soldiers. Certain of these sophisticated games allow
children to (10) _____ (*improvise, interface*) programs
of their own. Even when there is no set script, a child may
(11) _____ (*ad lib, debug*) a battle strategy. Therefore,
these games, rather than limiting the imagination, tend to
turn the mind into (12) _____ (an *extemporizing*,
a *confined*) instrument.

EXERCISE 4

Directions: On the lines in the following sentences, write the words in parentheses that *best fit the meanings* of the sentences.

1. When the student sits down in front of his computer, you might say he and his computer are _____ (*interfacing, alienating*).

2. The woman thought she had misunderstood the mechanic when he mentioned "bugs." In fact, he was seeking to fix her car or _____ (*input, debug*) it.

3. Today's computers are measured by how much _____ (*input, parody*) they can hold, how many bytes of information.

4. John thought his manager was asking him to throw the shotput when he spoke of throughput. In fact, he was concerned with his team's _____ (*silicon, productivity*).

5. It seems no matter how advanced our auto industry becomes, in the area of auto _____ (*output, silicone*), the Japanese continue to make gains.

6. One element that has revolutionized the computer industry is _____ (*plutonium, silicon*).

7. Woody Allen is an excellent comedian because he has the ability to _____ (*ad lib, protagonize*) on any occasion.

8. They say that former President Kennedy was able to _____ (*maximize, improvise*) at large press conferences.

9. Many people would not be walking today if it were not for the use of _____ (*silicon, silicone*) in artificial limbs.

10. Johnny Carson probably feels more at home when he speaks _____ (*thoughtfully, extemporaneously*) than when he has a script.

11. At one time, the term _____ (*scenario, parody*) was used mainly when referring to film scripts. Now it is used for almost any hypothetical situation.

12. There is the theory that a good play must have a strong _____ (*activist, protagonist*), one with whom the audience can identify.

13. Each Thanksgiving the schoolchildren put on a _____ (*parody, throughput*) of Gilbert and Sullivan's *Pirates of Penzance*.

Pretest 3

Directions: Match the words in column A with the meanings in column B. On the line, write the word from column B that is *closest in meaning*.

A	B

A

B

1. parsimonious _____ showing no emotion

2. niggardly _____ talkative

3. prodigal _____ drowsy, sluggish

4. altruistic _____ reduce severity

5. taciturn _____ work against

6. loquacious _____ silent, uncommunicative

7. apathetic _____ unselfishly devoted to others

8. lethargic _____ clever, inventive

9. militate _____ extravagant, profuse

10. mitigate _____ giving nothing, miserly

11. ingenious _____ unsophisticated, innocent

12. ingenuous _____ invalid

13. specious _____ apparently valid

14. plausible _____ stingy

Section IV, List 3

Do we have a sentence for you!

> In a marriage between a *parsimonious* man and a
> *prodigal* woman, the only solution is a conscien-
> tious development of *altruism*.

We'd better tackle one word at a time. The first one was
parsimonious. Any idea what it means? It doesn't seem to
resemble any familiar words. Does studying the context
help?

Probably one descriptive word means "stingy" and the
other means "extravagant," but any other speculation is
difficult.

> *Parsimonious* does mean "stingy," "mean about
> spending or giving even a small amount."

> A synonym is *niggardly*. They both mean "tight-
> fisted," but *niggardly* is more rigid in the idea of
> not giving anything.

> *Parsimonious* is defined as "frugality so extreme
> as to lead to stinginess," but the condemnation is
> not a severe one.

> *Prodigal* means "recklessly extravagant," "char-
> acterized by reckless, wasteful spending."

The combination of those traits would not lead to a
peaceful marriage. *Altruism* might be difficult to develop,
might be a difficult noncombat zone to establish.

> *Altruism* is the state of freedom from selfish
> interest, a lack of interest in any personal advan-

tage. It translates into an unselfish devotion to the welfare of others.

To reform one *parsimonious* spouse and one *prodigal* partner into an *altruistic* couple would take some doing!

Let's think of some other antonyms. Are *taciturn* and *loquacious* in your active vocabulary? You may know someone so *taciturn* that you just stop talking to him because you can never get more than a one-word answer. Trying to drag any details out of him isn't worth the effort. *Taciturn* people may be very lonely.

> *Taciturn* is defined as "temperamentally disinclined to talk." A synonym is "silent." The noun is *taciturnity*, "habitual silence."

> *Loquacious* is an antonym meaning "talkative." The noun is *loquaciousness*, "talkativeness."

What about *apathetic* and *lethargic*? Are they synonyms? They are used synonymously. The most observable trait of people who are *apathetic* or *lethargic* is indifference. The implications, the connotations, do vary slightly.

> Whereas *apathetic* means "showing little interest or emotion," *lethargic* adds the possibility of being drowsy because of disease or drugs.

Let's go back to malapropisms; they help sharpen communicating skills and awareness of clear vocabulary meanings. Correct this sentence:

> The strikers' attitude *mitigates* against an early settlement.

You've heard of *mitigating* circumstances. That doesn't seem to be the same meaning. The sentence needs something that means "prevents" or "works against." So we must have used *mitigates* as a malapropism.

You've been a successful sleuth again.

> *Mitigate* means to "soften the effect of," to "reduce the severity of." We might say that the widow's loneliness was *mitigated* by her volunteer activities.

What word did we need in the sentence about the strikers? *Militate*. That means to "operate or work against."

> Strong attitudes can *militate* against settlement. Associating the word with military and thinking of warfare may help keep them straight.

Another sentence:

> He received an early promotion because everyone admired his *ingenuousness*.

Meaning?

> *Ingenuous* means "innocent," "unsophisticated," maybe "childlike." We read about the *ingenuous* simplicity of the natives in uncivilized lands. It may also connote "honesty" because of innocence.

It's doubtful that a person so described would get an early promotion or be especially admired in the business world unless the business was show business. For our sentence, you need the word *ingenious*, meaning "clever," "original," "inventive."

> *Ingenious* also means "highly intelligent," maybe even "good at contriving." I have a neighbor who is *ingenious* at covering boxes to look like furniture. She shows much *ingenuity,* much originality and skill in carrying out her ideas.

A rather interesting variation is to add the prefix *dis* to *ingenuous*. It becomes *disingenuous* and is a restrained way to say "deceptive," "cheating."

> *Fortune* magazine once said, "The President was outraged by Brezhnev's *disingenuous* explanation." It just missed saying he had lied.

There is one more pair that you hear used interchangeably and may cause you to wonder if the speaker is certain of both meanings. They seem to overlap rather than to be synonyms or antonyms. The words are *specious* and *plausible*. They seem to mean almost the same thing. But they have slightly different connotations. Of the two, *specious* is a more hostile and assertive word.

> *Specious* humility has no sincere basis, nor do *specious* denials, even when they have an apparent validity.

It is defined as having a false look of truth. The noun is *speciousness*—the *speciousness* of the alibi.

There's also an adverb: *speciously,* meaning "showily," "deceptively."

Plausible refers to apparent validity. It casts some doubt but doesn't necessarily label the thing false.

A *plausible* argument is one that appears to be worthy of belief, is reasonably convincing but not proven.

Plausible leaves the door open for the possibility of being valid; *specious* does not.

Now let's review.

Parsimonious and *niggardly:* Stingy.

Prodigal: Extravagant.

Altruism: Unselfish devotion to others without any thought of personal gain.

Tactiturn and *loquacious:* Untalkative, and talkative, respectively.

Apathetic and *lethargic:* Indifferent, showing little interest; but *lethargic* may imply drowsiness caused by disease or drugs.

Next came the malapropisms *militate,* meaning to "work against," and *mitigate,* meaning to "soften the effect of."

Ingenious means "clever and inventive," and *ingenuous* means "innocent and unsophisticated."

> You may never have connected them before, but that's also where we get the term *ingenue*, meaning a "young woman in a play." That's what they always call the young star even when she isn't so innocent.

The last pair were *specious*, which means "definitely invalid," and *plausible*, which denotes a surface validity without proof.

> *Speciousness* includes an intent to defraud; *plausible* does not.

Now nail these down by completing Exercises 5 and 6 and Pretest 4. Then we'll discuss some incorrect pronunciations.

E X E R C I S E 5

Directions: On the lines in the following paragraph, write the words in parentheses that *best fit the meanings* of the sentences.

Radio, formerly known mainly as an outlet for music and news, has become filled with a (1) _____ (*prodigal*, *apathetic*) number of talk shows. In place of a (2) _____ (*taciturn*, *parsimonious*) announcer listing songs, we now have (3) _____ (*loquacious*, *specious*) personalities conversing on the (4) _____ (*altruism*, *activism*) of good citizens, the (5) _____ (*parsimony*, *acrimony*) of the city hall budget, and the (6) _____ (*niggardly*, *apathetic*) attitude of lazy teenagers. Not that all of these people are as (7) _____ (*taciturn*, *ingenious*) as they would have their listeners believe. In fact, many rely on (8) _____ (*niggardly*, *specious*) arguments to persuade the most (9) _____ (*parsimonious*, *lethargic*) of listeners to accept their points of view. Sometimes it is the caller who has a more questionable or even (10) _____ (*plausible*, *lethargic*) solution for a particular problem, whether it be to (11) _____ (*militate*, *mitigate*) the plight of the poor or to (12) _____ (*mitigate*, *militate*) against radical groups that are harming others. These talk-show gurus seem to be most (13) _____ (*niggardly*, *altruistic*) with their advice when they have to follow it themselves. One almost wishes for a return of the (14) _____ (*ingenuous*, *apathetic*) shows, heavy on music, light on talk.

EXERCISE 6

Directions: On the lines in the following sentences, write the words in parentheses that *best fit the meanings* of the sentences.

1. There are those who would rather be called _____ (*parsimonious, loquacious*) than feel they had to give to every good cause.

2. The man was so _____ (*niggardly, prodigal*) that he left the waitress a tip of three pennies.

3. It is the nature of youth to be _____ (*prodigal, taciturn*) in tipping to make a good impression.

4. America has a reputation of being _____ (*parsimonious, altruistic*) with smaller countries, having given huge amounts to develop resources and promote health.

5. Although communication is difficult, the _____ (*niggardly, taciturn*) person may possess great wisdom behind his silence.

6. On the other hand, one may be both _____ (*docile, loquacious*) and quite intelligent if one enjoys using many carefully selected words to explain one's ideas.

7. Sometimes it is in the nature of the philosopher to seem _____ (*apathetic, parsimonious*) when he is in fact deep in thought.

8. With a combined effort, the medical profession has been able to _____ (*excoriate, militate*) the inroads of cancer.

9. A wise parent will be able to _____ (*exacerbate, mitigate*) his child's feelings of despair.

10. If one tries to be _____ (*niggardly, ingenuous*), he may appear merely superficial, faking innocence.

11. By listening closely, the _____ (*ingenuous*, *specious*) nature of the money-making scheme can be detected.

12. Less than a generation ago it did not seem _____ (*importune*, *plausible*) that we would be able to land on the moon.

13. When Mary seemed most _____ (*lethargic*, *loquacious*) and quiet, many did not know she was taking a special drug for her asthma.

14. Gilbert was known for his _____ (*ingenuous*, *ingenious*) solutions to the continual problem of working without the recommended machinery.

Pretest 4

Directions: Match the words in column A with the meanings in column B. On the line, write the word from column B that is *closest in meaning*.

A	B
1. chic _____	midsection of body, stomach area
2. clique _____	cooked sugar sauce or confection
3. croissant _____	mature, full grown
4. caramel _____	crescent-shaped roll
5. abdomen _____	small fruit related to plum
6. adult _____	exclusive group
7. apricot _____	characteristic of North Pole, frigid
8. arctic _____	stylish, elegant
9. superfluous_____	extra, unnecessary

Section IV, List 4

Now we'll deal with pronunciations. Although regional pronunciations are more acceptable on broadcast media than they used to be, there are some pronunciations that are considered substandard. Two that are often noted are mispronunciations of *chic* and *clique*. A woman or a restaurant that is elegant, stylish, and sophisticated is not a baby chicken!

> They are *chic*, pronounced *sheek*.

> She dresses *chicly*, and the restaurant works hard to maintain an atmosphere of *chicness*.

Apparently the mispronunciation is the result of looking at the spelling without realizing that the word clings to its French ancestry.

An exclusive group that dines at that *chic* restaurant doesn't make clicking noises. They don't click; they belong to a *clique*, pronounced *cleek*.

> A *clique* is a group held together by common interests, views, and purposes. It excludes outsiders— whether in the high school lunchroom or the executive boardroom.

Another frequently used and often mispronounced word these days is the buttery pastry so popular in bakeries and coffeeshops. It's spelled *croissant* and correctly pronounced as an approach to if not a true French manner: *kwa-sań*. The translation, of course, is "crescent roll," because of the shape.

Almost as frequently mispronounced is *caramel*. It's often pronounced like the peninsula in California—Carmel—without that middle *a*.

> *Caramel* refers both to the brittle brown substance obtained by heating sugar for flavoring and coloring and to the chewy *caramel*-flavored candy.

> To *caramelize* is to change sugar into *caramel*.

If you eat *caramel* often, you obviously aren't considering the inches it can add to your *abdomen*—another often-mispronounced word. The accent should be on the beginning *ab*, not the *dom*.

One other mispronunciation that is prevalent in some areas is of the word *adult*, with the accent on the first syllable instead of the second. Although both are listed in dictionaries, the accent on the second syllable is the preferred choice—adulf.

How do you pronounce the fruit *apricot*?

Ápricot is the first choice, not with a long *a*. If most people in your region of the country use the second pronunciation given in the dictionary, it's certainly no crime to use it. In fact, you'll feel more comfortable. Do be sure it's an acceptable second choice, however. Knowing the first choice and using it may serve your purpose when you apply for a job as a radio announcer or a receptionist for someone who prefers careful attention to such details.

Another in that class is *arctic*. Many of us were taught to include that *k* sound. Now we hear it pronounced *art*.

That *k* sound may be on the way out. Strangely, when we use it to refer to the region around the North Pole or the type of frigid weather associated with it, the first pronunciation includes the *k* sound—*ark-tic*.

But when we use the same word to refer to an overshoe, the first pronunciation is *ar-tic*, without the *k*.

Those of us who use the *k* sound may have to change soon to be correct; it may not continue as the preferred pronunciation.

On the other hand, some pronunciations are not second-choice but are just plain wrong. One is *superfluous*, meaning "extra," "unnecessary." Current dictionaries agree that *super-fluous* is not acceptable; the accent is on *per*.

Let's pause now to complete Exercises 7 and 8 and Pretest 5. Then we'll continue with more prefixes and suffixes.

EXERCISE 7

Directions: On the lines in the following paragraph, write the words in parentheses that *best fit the meanings* of the sentences.

Philadelphia is undergoing a restaurant renaissance. There are more (1) _____ (*chic, clique*) restaurants than ever before. Of course, the (2) _____ (*croissant, apricot*) has become a common item to use in place of a roll, alone or with salad. While eating in these posh places with your particular (3) _____ (*clique, parody*), you must show some consideration for house specialties. Many feature desserts like chocolate cake with (4) _____ (*carmel, caramel*) icing. It would be poor taste and (5) _____ (*superfluous, opportune*) to engage in lengthy conversations about health foods with the waiter. Many of these eateries specialize in maintaining a style-conscious clientele that believes fashion is more important than warmth, even in (6) _____ (*arctic, artic*) temperatures.

EXERCISE 8

Directions: On the lines, write the *preferred pronunciations* for the following words.

1. chic (chick, sheek) _____
2. clique (klik, kleek) _____
3. croissant (kwa-sań, kroý-sent) _____
4. caramel (kar-mel, kar-a-mel) _____
5. abdomen (ab-dó-men, aб-do-men) _____
6. adult (a-dulf, aḍ-ult) _____
7. apricot (ăp-re-kot, āpe-re-kot) _____
8. arctic (North Pole) (ar-tik, ark-tik) _____
9. superfluous (su-peŕ-flu-us, su-per-flú-us) _____

Pretest 5

Directions: Match the prefixes and suffixes in column A with the meanings in column B. On the line, write the word from column B that is closest in meaning.

A	B
1. anti– _____	between
2. ante– _____	backward
3. inter– _____	against, opposed to
4. intra– _____	within
5. retro– _____	before, earlier
6. –less _____	state, quality, condition of
7. –ness, –hood, –dom _____	without, lacking
8. –ish _____	direction of
9. –ward _____	relating to, characteristic of

Section IV, List 5

One vocabulary aid we haven't included yet in this section is the use of prefixes and suffixes. But before we introduce some, let's review the prefixes we've had so far.

Can you remember those first ones we discussed that began with the letter *a*?

> We had *ab*, meaning "from," as in "abnormal," and *ad*, meaning "to" as in "adhere."

Then we have three beginning with *c*—not all introduced at the same time.

> The first was *com* or *con*, meaning "with," as in *compress*, meaning to "press with" or "together," and *converse*, meaning to "talk with."

> Introduced in another section were *circum*, meaning "around," as in *circumference*, and *contra*, meaning "against," as in *contradict*.

Now go for the *d*.

> *De* means "from," and we used *decelerate* as an example.

> *Dis* was the other. It means "apart" or "opposite," as in *disapprove* and *discourteous*.

We mentioned only one *e*—*ex*, meaning "from" or "out of," as in *excavate* and *exclude*.

How about those *i*s? Remember that the same prefix may have different meanings.

In can mean "in" or "into," as to *increase* or *induce*. But it can also mean "not."

So can *il, im,* and *ir.* Which one to use depends on the base word.

We have *invalid, illegal, immoral,* and *irregular.*

You're coming down the stretch now. There are three *p*'s.

Pre means "before"—*predict.*

Pro means "forward"—*promote.*

Pseudo means "fake," as in *pseudonym.*

Only an *r* and an *s* are left: *re* and *sub.*

Re means "back" or "again"—*react.*

Sub means "under," generally speaking—*subway.*

Now are the prefixes that indicate numbers:

"One" can be *uni* or *mono.*

"Two" is *bi.*

"Three" is *tri.*

"Four" is *quad.*

Multi is not a specific number but indicates "many."

Illustrative words are *unicorn, monotone, bicycle, tricycle, quadrangle,* and *multisensory.*

Now let's add some more. We mentioned *anto* when we were talking about *antonyms*. What is the usual meaning of the prefix *anti*? You were probably correct: "against." *Anto* is a variation of *anti*. Another meaning is "opposed to."

> We have *antifoaming* agents in our detergents, *antitoxins* to oppose the spread of disease, and *antirust* paint to guard our porch furniture.

However, we occasionally confuse *anti* with *ante*. Then our readers or listeners have trouble receiving our thoughts. *Ante* means "before," "prior," "earlier."

> To *antedate* a check is to predate it.

> The *anterior* end of an insect is the front.

> The hours before noon are designated A.M., meaning *ante meridiem*, "before the middle of the day."

Do you confuse *intra* and *inter*? *Inter* means "between." *Intra* means "within."

> *Intercollegiate* sports are between schools.

> *Intercity* means "between cities."

> *International* and *intercultural* mean "between nations" and "between cultures."

> *Intramural* means "within the walls."
> *Intramural* sports are within one school.

> *Intrapersonal* refers to something that happens within an individual. We read about *intrapersonal* concerns of the teenager.

Now one more that is a variation of one we discussed in the first section: *retro*. We had *re* meaning "again or back." *Retro* means "backward."

> A *retroactive* pay increase is active in past time, covers a period of time already passed.
>
> *Retrospect* refers to looking backward.
>
> *Retrorockets* produce thrust directly opposite to the motion of the craft, backward.

Fast review:

> *Anti* means "against"; *ante* means "before."
> *Inter* means "between"; *intra* means "within."
> *Retro* means "backward."

How about a few suffixes? What does *less* mean on the end of a word?

Perhaps it will be easier to think of the meaning when you use it in a word: *ageless* and *changeless*.

Now you know! It means without: "without age" or "without change." Thinking of a familiar word that uses a prefix or suffix, of course, aids in understanding meanings in words that are new to you.

Try this technique with *ness*.

> You know *kindness* and *happiness*. In those words, *ness* seems to mean "state of"—state of being kind or happy. Logically, it may also mean "amount" or "degree," as in *goodness*.

How about *ish*?

> You might think of *boyish* or *slavish*. Then you
> speculate that the suffix means "characteristic
> of" or "associated with"—characteristic of a boy
> or of a slave.

> It implies that it is typical of the associated thing,
> as in *boyish*.

> It also denotes "approximately," as in *fivish* mean-
> ing "approximately five o'clock" and *fortyish*
> meaning "near forty years old."

Then there are *hood* and *dom*, also meaning "state" or
"condition" or "character of."

> *Childhood, falsehood*, and *likelihood* all indicate
> those conditions.

> The *dom* in *serfdom, freedom*, and *boredom* mean
> those states of being.

There's one more that seems to fit with this group: *ward*,
meaning "in the direction of."

> *Backward, homeward*, and *forward* are three words
> that use that suffix and indicate direction to "back,"
> "home," and "ahead."

That brings up another confusion: what's the difference
between *forward* and *foreword*?

> *Forward* means "belonging to the front part,"
> "moving ahead," or "sending onward." It also
> indicates the basketball player who plays in front.

Foreword means a "word in front." It's usually more than one word, written by an author to explain what he or she has written, and it appears in the front of a book.

Reviewing suffixes:

Less means "without" or "lacking."

Ness means "state," "quality," or "condition of."

Ish means "relating to" or "characteristic of."

Hood and *dom* mean the "state or condition of."

Ward means "direction of."

Now it's time to practice. As we recommended at the end of the previous sections, now is a good time to look back over the written exercises in this section to clarify any confusion and erase any uncertainty.

Previously we suggested considering all the parts of speech associated with a word to help you review it. Another technique is to find how many words can be used to describe or take the place of one selected noun. For example:

Using the noun *word*, go down the list of words to find how many can either modify it or take its place.

With words we can *abnegate, circumvent, connote, corroborate, denote, deprecate, depreciate, disparage, elucidate, imply,* and *infer.*

Go back to see if you know the meaning, the result if your words do each of those things. Can you get a clear mental image of the denotations and connotations? Can you use any to relieve the overworked "said"?

Now complete Exercises 9 and 10. When you feel you've mastered this section, proceed to Section V.

EXERCISE 9

Directions: On the lines in the following sentences, write
the prefixes or suffixes that *best fit the meanings* of the
sentences.

1. The paint included an _____*rust* agent to prevent
   corrosion.
2. _____*spect* often adds knowledge you didn't have
   when the event occurred.
3. His eternally *boy*_____ face made it easy for
   him to keep his true age a secret.
4. The _____*cultural* exchange worked well in theory
   but presented challenges in practice.
5. The banker disapproved of his wife's _____*dating*
   her checks to avoiding paying the penalty.
6. He had expected his vacation home to preserve the
   *change*_____ monotony of boredom he'd known
   as a child.
7. The art show was limited to _____*mural* selections
   of enrolled students.
8. The degree of *good*_____ of the benefits may
   depend on what the individual already has and needs.
9. His *for*_____ direction was halted by a tackle.

EXERCISE 10

Directions: Answer the questions on the lines provided.

1. Which prefix means "backward"? _____
2–4. Which three suffixes mean "state" or "quality of"?
_____   _____   _____
5. Which prefix means "before"? _____
6. What is the prefix meaning "opposed to" or "against"?
_____
7. What suffix means "relating to," "characteristic of"?
_____
8. "Direction of" is the meaning of what suffix?
_____
9. The prefix of the word *intrapersonal* has what meaning? _____
10. Which suffix means "without," "lacking"? _____

ANSWER KEY—SECTION IV

Pretest 1

1. individual speech pattern
2. regional speech pattern
3. conversational expression
4. slang or specialized vocabulary
5. location
6. gift recipient
7. legal document
8. addition to a will
9. agent of change
10. aggravate, make worse
11. denounce, remove skin
12. outstanding
13. treelike

Exercise 1

1. jargon
2. dialect
3. beneficiary
4. codicil
5. exacerbated
6. excoriate
7. colloquialisms
8. stellar
9. brief
10. catalyst
11. venue
12. arboreal

Exercise 2

1. individual speech pattern
2. conversational expression
3. location
4. gift recipient
5. addition to legal document
6. agent of change
7. aggravate, make worse
8. regional speech
9. legal document
10. denounce
11. outstanding
12. of a tree
13. specialized vocabulary

Pretest 2

1. work together, communicate
2. remove errors
3. information entered
4. productivity
5. result
6. nonmetallic element used in compounds
7. organic compound used in lubricants
8. as desired, freely
9. make up on the spot
10. without notes
11. plot outline
12. leading character
13. imitation of style

Exercise 3

1. Silicon
2. silicone
3. interfacing
4. debug
5. input
6. throughput
7. scenario
8. protagonist
9. parody
10. improvise
11. ad lib
12. an extemporizing

Exercise 4

1. interfacing
2. debug
3. input
4. productivity
5. output
6. silicon
7. ad lib
8. improvise
9. silicone
10. extemporaneously
11. scenario
12. protagonist
13. parody

Pretest 3

1. stingy
2. giving nothing, miserly
3. extravagant, profuse
4. unselfishly devoted to others
5. silent, uncommunicative
6. talkative
7. showing no emotion
8. drowsy, sluggish
9. work against
10. reduce severity
11. clever, inventive
12. unsophisticated, innocent
13. invalid
14. apparently valid

Exercise 5

1. prodigal
2. taciturn
3. loquacious
4. altruism
5. parsimony
6. apathetic
7. ingenious
8. specious
9. lethargic
10. plausible
11. mitigate
12. militate
13. niggardly
14. ingenuous

Exercise 6

1. parsimonious
2. niggardly
3. prodigal
4. altruistic
5. taciturn
6. loquacious
7. apathetic
8. militate
9. mitigate
10. ingenuous
11. specious
12. plausible
13. lethargic
14. ingenious

Pretest 4

1. stylish, elegant
2. exclusive group
3. crescent-shaped roll
4. cooked sugar sauce or confection
5. midsection of body, stomach area
6. mature, full-grown
7. small fruit related to plum
8. characteristic of North Pole, frigid
9. extra, unnecessary

Exercise 7

1. chic
2. croissant
3. clique
4. caramel
5. superfluous
6. arctic

Exercise 8

1. sheek
2. kleek
3. kwa-sań
4. kar-a-mel
5. aḃ-do-men
6. a-dulf
7. ăp-re-kot
8. ark-tik
9. su-peŕ-flu-us

Pretest 5

1. against, opposed to
2. before, earlier
3. between
4. within
5. backward
6. without, lacking
7. state, quality, condition of
8. relating to, characteristic of
9. direction of

Exercise 9

1. antirust
2. retrospect
3. boyish
4. intercultural
5. antedating
6. changeless
7. intramural
8. goodness
9. forward

Exercise 10

1. retro
2–4. ness, hood, dom
5. ante
6. anti
7. ish
8. ward
9. within
10. less

SECTION V

SECTION V

This is the last section, and there are so many words left to examine! We've barely dented the eight-hundred-thousand estimate. Again, we must be selective, knowing that we can choose only a few representative groups to help you communicate more clearly and quickly.

What kinds of words do you find present the most consistent problems when you're searching for just the right way to communicate a particular thought?

Although we can't hear your answer, answers we *have* heard plead for more descriptive words, more new ways to describe without repeating the overused ones. There are many that vary just slightly. They literally color your nouns and verbs to give the vivid mental pictures that you want your listeners and readers to receive. Those descriptive words are some of the hardest to nail in place.

Before we begin, please complete Pretest 1 for Section V now. (See p. 242 for the correct answers to the tests and exercises in this section.)

Pretest 1

Directions: Match the words in column A with the meanings in column B. On the line, write the word from column B that is *closest in meaning*.

A	B
1. ecstatic _____	pleasant, appropriate
2. enraptured _____	lively, animated
3. flamboyant _____	balky, contrary
4. vivacious _____	evil, corrupt
5. felicitous _____	showy, colorful
6. restive _____	overwhelmed by emotion
7. depraved _____	overly mournful
8. lugubrious _____	peevish, nagging
9. querulous _____	ill-natured, upsetting
10. bilious _____	extremely delighted

Section V, List 1

Now let's discuss words that describe pleasant emotions or responses to them. What is the meaning of *ecstatic*?

It means "overwhelmed with delight." It even implies being beyond reason and self-control. The noun is *ecstasy,* and an old idea even included swooning from the strong emotion.

It refers to any overwhelming emotion. To be *ecstatically* happy is the most frequent use, with *enraptured* being one synonym.

Romantic novels frequently have *enraptured* heroines responding *ecstatically* to advances by the heroes. Not many of them swoon anymore, but the potential is there.

Children may become *ecstatic* during the excitement of Christmas. When they are completely *enraptured*, completely absorbed in delight and intense emotion, parents have difficulty communicating unrelated ideas like eating and sleeping.

Both words—*ecstatic* and *enraptured*—are also used to describe an intense emotional reaction to a spiritual experience. Then the result may be a trance, a not necessarily pleasant state of being totally unaware of surroundings.

You may associate it with *flamboyant* behavior—not run-of-the-mill reactions to everyday events. *Flamboyant* is another good adjective to describe a very colorful display of emotion. Again, the emotion could also be unpleasant.

With *flamboyant*, the emphasis is on the striking display of the emotion. In fact, the root word means to "flame"—the same root as our old friend *flammable*. So *flamboyant* behavior is flaming behavior—and that's noticeable!

You might even say it's *vivacious* behavior.

Vivacious means being "lively," "animated," "filled with *vivacity*," "filled with life and vigor." It is often associated with youthful enthusiasm, but older citizens can be *vivacious* too. The association is with life, not necessarily age. The root word means to "live."

Let's get away from the overactive display of emotion. *Felicitous* seems to fit lots of places, and it's pleasant.

> It means "pleasant," "delightful." *Felicity* means the "state of being happy"—especially great happiness. It can also refer to something that causes happiness.

> A fellow worker might say that your contribution to a major project is *felicitous,* meaning "appropriate" and "showing *felicity*." If he *felicitates* you on that appropriateness, he is congratulating you.

This word deals with pleasantness in all its meanings and connotations. It may even refer to a pleasing manner or quality in art or language. No bad vibes there!

Sometimes we need to describe the baddies, too. You may read of a character described as *restive*. Is that good or bad? When you look it up, you'll find it means "stubbornly resisting control," "balky." Such a character is noticed by restlessness, nervousness, constant movement.

An even less desirable role to play would be that of a *depraved* character.

> *Depraved* means "incorrigibly evil," "corrupt." If your character *depraved* someone else, he would corrupt him or her morally.

> *Depravity* may be a corrupt act or practice. The old-time villain who made heartless demands on the ingenuous heroine was *depraved,* had a warped sense of justice.

And the hero was always *lugubriously* upset about the whole thing—really overdid the reaction by being ridiculously mournful and sorrowful. It's fun doing a melodrama like that; exaggeration rules! The actors can really ham it up being overly mournful, *lugubrious*.

Both *querulous* and *bilious* describe unpleasant characters.

> *Querulous* means "peevish, nagging." Querulous people are noted for their habitual whining and complaining. Unfortunately for mothers-in-law, the typecasting of those ladies has long noted their *querulousness*, their ability to respond to any situation *querulously*.

You probably thought *bilious* referred to bile from the liver. It does.

> The first meaning in the dictionary is "suffering from disordered liver function." But from there, the meaning moved to "appearing as if affected by a bilious disorder." The next step was easy: "of a peevish, ill-natured disposition."

So it's another from the medical background. It's often used to refer to an unpleasant, upsetting, disturbing color associated with the same condition, as in a *bilious* color that apparently accompanies *biliousness*.

Let's do a quick review in the pleasant category.

> *Ecstatic* and *enraptured*: Overpowered by delight.

> *Flamboyant*: Inflamed action and reaction, noticeable dramatics, and probably including *vivacity*, liveliness, and animation.

> *Felicitous*: Pleasant and appropriate.

Next we had the so-called baddies:

Restive: Restless and nervous.

Depraved: Evil and corrupt.

Querulous: Peevish and nagging.

Lugubrious: Overplaying the mournful bit.

Bilious: Having a sour stomach or bad temper, or both.

What's next? Some written practice before we continue with styles of communicating. Please complete Exercises 1 and 2 and Pretest 2.

EXERCISE 1

Directions: On the lines in the following paragraph, write the words in parentheses that *best fit the meanings* of the sentences.

Psychologists warn us that at the beginning of each new year there may be a tendency to slip into a (1) _____ (*lugubrious*, *ecstatic*) state. After the (2) _____ (*ecstatic*, *depraved*) period of the Christmas season, followed by a (3) _____ (*lugubrious*, *flamboyant*) New Year's Eve party, a letdown is to be expected. Back to earth, we become (4) _____ (*enraptured*, *restive*) and (5) _____ (*vivacious*, *querulous*) over little things. Some say a return to nature will rekindle that (6) _____ (*enraptured*, *restive*) Christmas spirit. After a brisk walk in the woods, one feels (7) _____ (*vivacious*, *querulous*) and ready for (8) _____ (*felicitous*, *lugubrious*) conversation. Gone are those (9) _____ (*depraved*, *ecstatic*) thoughts about blowing up the world to end the winter blahs. After a visit to the spa or an afternoon of ice skating, we even begin to talk to the Browns, our ill-natured, (10) _____ (*ecstatic*, *bilious*) neighbors.

210 Learn, Inc.

EXERCISE 2

Directions: On the lines in the following sentences, write the words in parentheses that *best fit the meanings* of the sentences.

1. When the child found the long-wanted skates under the Christmas tree, he was _____ (*ecstatic, lugubrious*).
2. Although Van Gogh's behavior was often showy and _____ (*flamboyant, taciturn*), his paintings showed great control over his art.
3. A _____ (*vivacious, bilious*) teacher, full of smiles, often receives similar looks from her students.
4. Even though the daughter was apathetic, the mother had a most _____ (*felicitous, depraved*) interest in helping solve the neighborhood problem.
5. If one watches a series of horror films, _____ (*depraved, enraptured*) characters may appear to be acceptable.
6. People seem to be most _____ (*restive, ecstatic*) when it is raining and on Mondays.
7. The _____ (*lugubrious, querulous*) expression on the clown's face is offset by his zany antics.
8. When Henry Higgins complained of being _____ (*bilious, restive*), he was referring to his liver, not his disposition.
9. Some customers become so _____ (*querulous, enraptured*) over a minor detail that the salesperson would prefer to lose the sale and leave them alone.
10. There is something about the first snowfall of winter that leaves us _____ (*enraptured, depraved*) with its beauty.

Pretest 2

Directions: Match the words in column A with the meanings in column B. On the line, write the word from column B that is *closest in meaning*.

A	B
1. obsequious _____	moralizing
2. decorous _____	fluent, possibly insincere
3. garrulous _____	inflexible, immovable
4. loquacious _____	wordy
5. verbose _____	restrained, reluctant
6. glib _____	discursively talkative
7. sententious _____	concise, brief
8. adamant _____	inflated, padded
9. reticent _____	loud
10. laconic _____	pointlessly talkative
11. bombastic _____	submissive, obedient
12. vociferous _____	waver, sway
13. vacillate _____	proper

Section V, List 2

You're quite right, of course, in believing that the descriptive words you use make a big difference in the way your reader or listener receives the message you intend. We have too many words that leave a great deal of room for interpretation—not only connotations that we've been discussing, but words that have indefinite meanings. They're not necessarily long or difficult words, but their meanings aren't clear without some frame of reference.

What happened to succinct writing? Does it sound like we're suggesting using more words instead of fewer?

If that was what you were thinking, you just made our point. "More" than how many? The fewest number to keep an exchange of words going, or the fewest number to send a clear message? To illustrate, how many are "too many" or "too few"? And who is to determine exactly the number that constitutes "too many"?

Being succinct in not using more words than are necessary does not mean using so few words that there is room for interpretation. For example, how might a listener interpret your meaning when you returned from hearing a famous speaker and said that he spoke "too long"?

The general idea would be clear: he should have stopped sooner. However, the reason would have to be a guess. Maybe the last part of his speech added nothing to your understanding of his subject. It could also mean that he spoke longer than you wanted to listen. Perhaps he went on longer than advance publicity led you to believe he would. Or... You're beginning to see what we mean.

You can think of at least five other messages you might receive: The speaker presented material you already knew; made you physically uncomfortable by forcing you to sit so long; prevented you from shopping for a birthday gift on your way home; added too much irrelevant material; or left no time for the speaker scheduled to follow him. All these and many more are possible.

Ideally, in any communication process you foresee possible misinterpretations and prevent them before they happen. That requires that you be mentally alert and make a practice of being aware of the roadblocks to clear meaning. Do a mental check on how your words can be received, and add the words necessary to keep your intent very clear.

There are two acronyms to help us remember the importance of clarity. We have KISS (Keep It Simple, Stupid) and KICS (Keep It Clear and Simple). Acronyms make words from initial letters of words and serve as useful mnemonics.

How about some more words to describe communication styles?

Some inexperienced people act *obsequiously*, and that never helps them accomplish their goals for communicating.

> If they're *obsequious* they exhibit no assertiveness at all, acting like a servant wanting to please, even fawning. Synonyms are "dutiful," "submissive," "obedient," "compliant."
>
> *Obsequiousness* means "attentiveness," "slavish submission." Students desiring undeservedly good grades may be *obsequious* until the end of the semester. So may employees hoping for the next promotion.

It means going further than just being *decorous*.

> *Decorous* means "acting with *decorum*," with good taste and appropriateness for polite behavior. The emphasis is on being correct, not in acting subservient.

When you communicate *decorously,* you are absolutely proper. The queen, for example, must always be aware of what is *decorous* for the situation, since she is always the focus of attention.

Those who serve her act *obsequiously*. They may be sincere in their desire to please her, but there is often a connotation of having some selfish motive in mind.

They would control any tendency to be *garrulous* when she was present. Being too talkative may show a lack of respect or obsequiousness.

While *garrulous* means "talkative," it includes the idea of being pointless and annoying. It implies "rambling without any great contribution to the listener." A synonym is *loquacious*. Both mean "wordy without content."

Another synonym for "wordy" is *verbose*, which places the emphasis on using an excessive number of words. A *verbose* speaker is one who takes an hour for a half-hour message. You've undoubtedly heard him or her.

To review those three almost-synonyms:

Garrulous means "habitually talkative." *Loquacious* means "excessively talkative," perhaps "discursive."

Verbose means "using an excessive number of words." A synonym for all three is "wordy."

Where does *glib* fit in to the picture?

Glib means "quickness or fluency in speaking or writing that suggests insincerity."

Glib replies are usually nonchalant, offhand. *Glib* politicians may be suspected of showing little thought or concern for their constituents.

Sententious is the other side of the picture, but it may be no more commendable. A *sententious* speaker may be more succinct, but what is said abounds in excessive moralizing. A *sententious* speaker is not *loquacious*. He or she expresses many pithy thoughts in few words and is fond of proverbs, maxims, and famous sayings and quotations. As opposed to *glib* often being used to describe an insincere sales staff, *sententious* is often used to describe the clergy.

It might mean that they're *adamant*, but the words are not synonyms.

> *Adamant* means "inflexible," "immovable." Its root refers to an impenetrably hard stone—in fact, that's the first meaning. We use it as an adjective to mean "firm in purpose and opinion," "unyielding"—especially in opposition.

That leads us to styles that get in the way of communication—or at least, styles of expression that make communication difficult. What's an antonym for "talkative"?

There's *taciturn*, which we already discussed, and *reticent*, which means "reserved," "inclined to be silent," "uncommunicative."

> *Reticent* may even mean "restrained in appearance." Sometimes it's used to mean "reluctant," as in *reticent* about expressing an opinion. The usual synonym is "silent."

Then there's *laconic*.

Laconic doesn't necessarily imply a *reticence* to speak; it just means "concise"—sometimes to the point of rudeness. It was used to describe the ancient Spartans, who were known for their brevity of speech. When Philip of Macedon wrote to them, "If I enter your city, I will raze it to the ground," their magistrates sent back the *laconic* answer: "If."

> *Laconism* means "succinctness of expression." Some stand-up comedians are known for their *laconic* wit; they use one-liners instead of long shaggy-dog stories.

Would you consider *bombastic* an antonym?

If you answered "yes," you are correct. *Bombast* means "padded, inflated communication." It comes from a word meaning "cotton padding" and stresses the inflation of style. However, it doesn't rule out the possibility of substantial content. The inflation isn't necessarily hot air, but the style is hardly succinct. Orators are *bombastic;* most good speakers lean toward being succinct.

Where does *vociferous* enter this picture?

Vociferous concentrates on quantity of sound, not quality of content—usually with more decibels than necessary. It may be associated with shouting, often in disagreement and always to get attention.

Question: Would someone using a *vociferous* style of communicating be apt to be *vacillating*?

"No way!" is the answer to that one. *Vacillating* thinkers waver back and forth without being able to stick to one opinion or one course of action. They'd never say anything *vociferously* because that would imply a firm stand.

> A *vacillating* speaker leaves you wondering what action is being suggested.

Vacillating also means "physically wavering back and forth," "swaying from side to side."

Let's review the ways of communicating clearly or unclearly.

Obsequious: Wanting only to serve, servile for whatever reason.

Decorous: Appropriate or polite and proper.

Garrulous: Talkative.

Loquacious: Wordy, maybe rambling.

Verbose: Wordy, as in using too many words.

Glib: Fluent but maybe insincere.

Sententious: Succinct but moralizing.

Adamant: Inflexible.

Now the next group about communication:

Reticent: Reluctant.

Laconic: Brief.

Bombastic: Inflated.

Vociferous: Loud.

Vacillating: Wavering—physically or mentally.

We'll continue after you've completed Exercises 3 and 4 and Pretest 3.

EXERCISE 3

Directions: On the lines in the following paragraphs, write
the words in parentheses that *best fit the meanings* of the
sentences.

The speech teacher asked the students to prepare a reading
of the (1) _____ (*vacillating, glib*) speech that Hamlet
delivered so smoothly to the players, "Speak the speech, I
pray you, as I pronounced it to you."

One student complained that the writing was (2) _____
(*bombastic, reticent*). However, the teacher was (3) _____
(*adamant, vacillating*) about the selection.

Miss Bramin read the words correctly, but the volume of her
voice seemed to (4) _____ (*vociferate, vacillate*) like
an old summer fan. Mr. Parks was so (5) _____
(*vociferous, glib*) that the room filled with the echoes of his
voice bouncing off the walls. Then Miss Warner spoke in
such a (6) _____ (*reticent, bombastic*) manner that not
even those in the front row could hear her. Mr. Quick added
several speeches of his own, making the entire selection a
(7) _____ (*reticent, verbose*) tapestry, unintelligible to
all. Mr. Swift, standing in a (8) _____ (*glib, decorous*)
way and avoiding the (9) _____ (*reticent, sententious*)
or preachy quality of the others, gave a fine reading. Finally,
the shy, (10) _____ (*obsequious, flamboyant*) Miss
Parsley spoke in a whisper, leaving those in the back to
wonder if she were doing the reading in mime. The teacher
left with this (11) _____ (*garrulous, laconic*) message: "Class dismissed." Class members discussed the dan-
gers in being too talkative as in (12) _____ (*loquacious, laconic*), especially in rambling aimlessly or (13)
_____ (*sententiously, garrulously*).

EXERCISE 4

Directions: On the lines in the following sentences, write the words in parentheses that *best fit the meanings* of the sentences.

1. Jeremy decided that if he was _____ (*obsequious*, *adamant*), the policeman would give him only a warning ticket.

2. The _____ (*decorous*, *laconic*) furniture in the White House is pleasing to the eye.

3. A _____ (*garrulous*, *reticent*) person becomes obnoxious when he will not let anyone else speak.

4. If one has a pleasant voice and a wealth of information to share, the habit of being overly _____ (*vacillating*, *loquacious*) will be endured.

5. A radio announcer usually possesses a _____ (*glib*, *dour*) tongue.

6. Polonius, in *Hamlet*, is one of the most _____ (*laconic*, *sententious*) of stage characters, endlessly dispensing good advice and righteous judgment.

7. If one is always _____ (*adamant*, *decorous*) and inflexible with a teenage child, the results can be rebellion.

8. At a dinner party, there is always that moment of decision: to be _____ (*bombastic*, *reticent*) or begin a conversation with the stranger sitting next to you.

9. Many would agree that Hemingway's prose style is _____ (*garrulous*, *laconic*) and concise.

10. The wording of a tax bill was considered _____ (*bombastic*, *decorous*), inflated, padded, even by those who supported the legislation.

11. Some people feel that if they are _____ (*reticent*, *vociferous*) enough, they can wear down an adversary.

12. The _____ (*vacillating*, *adamant*) nature of Hamlet was best expressed in his famous soliloquy, "To be or not to be, that is the question."

13. Many young writers tend to be _____ (*verbose*, *decorous*) and thus have to shorten their work.

Pretest 3

Directions: Match the words in column A with the meanings in column B. On the line, write the word from column B that is *closest in meaning*.

	A	B
1.	dour _____	irritable, easily angered
2.	blasé _____	obstinate, defiant
3.	odious _____	practical
4.	pragmatic _____	being or doing evil
5.	recalcitrant _____	doing good
6.	irascible _____	enjoying people
7.	malevolent _____	offensive, deserving hatred
8.	benevolent _____	cynic
9.	misanthrope _____	worldly, bored
10.	gregarious _____	stern, sullen

Section V, List 3

Other descriptive words provide exact descriptions of various types of people. Let's get into those.

One is *dour,* and the preferred pronunciation is with an *au* sound in the middle.

Dour means "stern," "harsh," "obstinate,"
"unyielding," "gloomy," "sullen." A *dour* man
is always silent and bad-tempered.

What is a *blasé* person?

We often think of it as meaning "worldly and sophisticated." We might like that description applied to us. But I
don't think you'll desire the rest of the description: "apathetic
to pleasure or excitement." The connection, of course, is
that of being uninterested because of frequent exposure to
exciting things. You'll have to wait until you get bored with
the joy of each day to be truly *blasé*.

Boredom is often considered especially *odious*, especially
worthy of blame, because boredom is considered a controll-
able state of mind, one that can be eliminated.

Odious means "deserving hatred." When a business or an association with certain people is
labeled *odious*, it is abhorrent to the speaker.

Odium is the disgrace that comes from hateful
conduct, conduct deserving contempt. The dictionary definition for *odium* is very strong: "hatred
and condemnation accompanied by loathing or
contempt."

You can't get much nastier than that! So, *odious* company
certainly is not the kind you seek!

On the other hand, you may not want to be considered
pragmatic. That means "concerned with practical matters."
The implication is of being concerned with practical matters
to the exclusion of intellectual or artistic matters. In fact,
there's an American movement in philosophy founded by
C. S. Pierce and William James called *Pragmatism*. Its

basis is that the function of thought is to guide action, and all truth should be tested by the practical consequences of belief. You don't have to know all that, but it may help you remember the word.

There are three more disagreeable words that may be useful: *recalcitrant, irascible,* and *malevolent.*

> *Recalcitrant* is a little like *adamant.* They both mean "unbending." But while *adamant* means "unbending," *recalcitrant* means "obstinate," "defiant of authority," "unruly," "hard to manage."
>
> A *recalcitrant* child may be disobedient and stubbornly resist guidance.

One child displaying *recalcitrance* may lead a brother or sister to be *irascible,* which means "irritable," "easily angered." *Irascibility* is demonstrated by a hot temper and quick anger.

Malevolence refers to the malice that may result from consistently *recalcitrant* or *irascible* behavior. *Malevolence* arises from intense ill will, spite, or hatred. It often produces more of the same. A *malevolent* person can be an evil influence.

On the other hand, *benevolence* is just the opposite. Even in despots. Remember the term *benevolent despot* in history books when the ruler with absolute power was concerned with the welfare of his subjects?

> *Benevolence* is the inclination to do good or even the act of kindness or the gift itself.
>
> All fairy godmothers are *benevolent.*

Another aside: *benevolence* was also a tax levied by some English kings without the authority of Parliament. The kings preferred to consider that income a gift.

At least they weren't *misanthropes*.

A *misanthropic* person is also cynical. When you feel you can't trust anyone, you don't look forward to much that is happy. Your communication lines wouldn't exactly be open, either. You'd have no desire to associate with other people or to join groups if you were convinced no one could be trusted.

A *misanthrope* couldn't possibly be very *gregarious*. *Gregariousness* includes enjoying people and their company. That whole idea would be lost to *misanthropes*.

Let's go back and take a look at the cast of characters we've put on stage. It certainly is varied!

Dour: Gloomy, obstinate, sullen.

Blasé: No longer interested in excitement or pleasure, often by overexposure to such things. Sophisticated.

Odious: Deserving contempt or blame.

Recalcitrant: Defiant of authority.

Irascible: Irritable.

Malevolent and benevolent: Filled with malice, and kind and doing good, respectively.

Gregarious: Refers to the joiner, the inveterate club member who enjoys the company of other people.

Now, for written practice, complete Exercises 5 and 6 and Pretest 4. When you're comfortable with that impressive array of characters, join us for words used to describe physical characteristics of people.

EXERCISE 5

Directions: On the lines in the following paragraph, write the words in parentheses that *best fit the meanings* of the sentences.

When going away to college for the first time, one of the biggest adjustments is meeting a whole new set of people. On the same floor of your dorm you may find (1) _____ (a *dour*, an *ecstatic*) long-faced science major rooming with a worldly, (2) _____ (*blasé*, *decorous*) English-lit buff. The language at one end of the corridor may be coarse and (3) _____ (*odious*, *benevolent*) while at the other end there is a healthy sense of (4) _____ (*benevolent*, *odious*) mutual aid. Then, too, at your dining table you may be surrounded by friendly, (5) _____ (*adamant*, *gregarious*) faces, only to see at the end of the table the biggest (6) _____ (*benefactor*, *misanthrope*) on campus trying to dampen everyone else's enjoyment. Thankfully, there will not be a large number of deadbeat, (7) _____ (*felicitous*, *recalcitrant*) people. Most college students are ready to learn and tend not to be on the (8) _____ (*irascible*, *enraptured*), irritable side. The problem with most will not be a temptation to a (9) _____ (*malevolent*, *benevolent*) way to annoy others but how to use their own time. Even though college can be fun, it must be realized that one is there for the (10) _____ (*odious*, *pragmatic*) preparation for the future.

EXERCISE 6

Directions: On the lines in the following sentences, write the words in parentheses that *best fit the meanings* of the sentences.

1. Was there ever a more _____ (*vivacious*, *dour*) character than Scrooge in *The Christmas Carol*?

2. Often the _____ (*blasé*, *odious*) person is inwardly not as sophisticated as he or she acts.

3. For those over forty, rock lyrics seem to contain more _____ (*odious*, *pragmatic*) language than the songs of the 1950s.

4. Even though Edison had a great imagination, he was very _____ (*gregarious*, *pragmatic*) when it came to making his inventions functional.

5. The _____ (*benevolent*, *recalcitrant*) youngster rejected each dish at the dinner table and even refused to taste what he had ordered.

6. One who becomes an _____ (*irascible*, *ecstatic*) adult has often grown up in a hostile environment.

7. The _____ (*blasé*, *malevolent*) nature of nuclear warfare was given a disastrous preview at Hiroshima.

8. If given a chance, the _____ (*irascible*, *benevolent*) side of people will usually come to the fore when help is needed.

9. At holiday time, people seem more _____ (*recalcitrant*, *gregarious*) and friendly than at any other time of the year.

10. Sometimes the person considered to be a _____ (*misanthrope*, *pragmatist*) is simply too honest with his assessment of the faults of others.

Pretest 4

Directions: Match the words in column A with the meanings in column B. On the line, write the word from column B that is *closest in meaning*.

A	B
1. corpulent _____	vigor, energy
2. obese _____	beauty
3. flaccid _____	wise
4. maimed _____	slow, sluggish, cowlike
5. bovine _____	keen insight
6. pulchritude _____	disabled
7. virility _____	wise caution
8. sagacious _____	judging wisely
9. acumen _____	all-knowing
10. prudence _____	fat
11. judicious _____	bulky
12. omniscient _____	flabby, weakened

Section V, List 4

It seems the main description we read of people these days is *corpulent*. Surely the whole world isn't fat!

Perhaps we're just changing our standards of how *obese* we can be and still maintain good health as we know about the types of foods we must eat to prolong our lives.

> *Corpulent* does, of course, mean "of large bulk." *Obese* is a synonym. The nouns are *obesity* and *corpulence*. Although they're used interchangeably, *obesity* is more apt to be used to describe the condition caused by overeating.

Both also imply the presence of *flaccid* muscles. That means the mighty sag—flabby and even weak from the energy needed to lug all that bulk around without proper muscle tone.

Let's look at another word: *maimed*. *Maimed* has been displaced in most common usage by *disabled*, but it's a good word to mean specifically "disabled by the loss of a limb." It is also used as a verb to mean to "disfigure or disable by depriving of use of a limb."

Crippled is rarely used because it has a derogatory connotation—another example of how the implied meanings change.

Bovine, coming from the Latin word for "cow," is a useful descriptive word for slow, sluggish people. You can picture them contentedly grazing all day without any desire to conquer the world beyond their fences. Another dull one!

Let's get to more pleasant people! Let's consider *pulchritude* and *virility*.

> *Pulchritude* means "physical beauty," "attractive-ness," and most people enjoy viewing it. The Miss America contest has tried to include other considerations, such as talent, charm, and the ability to think, but the word *pulchritude* means "beauty." It comes from the Latin root meaning "beautiful."

Besides being handsome, today's dream-fulfilling man must be masculine and vigorous: in a word, *virile*.

> It even implies "energetic" and "forceful."
>
> *Virility* includes the idea of sexual potency as well—the ideal macho man or jock, to use currently popular terms.

Leaving the beautiful scene, *sagacious* is another favorable descriptive word.

> *Sagacious* means "wise." A person who is *sagacious* may be known as a *sage*.
>
> A *sage* is someone who is respected for his wisdom and calm judgment.
>
> *Sagacious* means "keen insight," too. You are undoubtedly a *sagacious* judge of character and show *sagacity* in stock purchases. That means you're shrewd and discerning.

That may also mean you have *acumen*, and that includes having keen insight.

However, the emphasis with *sagacity* is "wisdom and sound judgment" from past experience.

Acumen is almost intuitional penetration of a problem combined with keen practical judgment. Then there's *prudence*, that's very similar. How would you distinguish it?

> Someone who is *prudent* is wisely cautious, especially wise in handling practical matters when it's important to consider all the consequences.
>
> A *prudent* company treasurer wouldn't invest all the company funds in one place, no matter what his intuition might lead him to do with his personal money.
>
> A *prudent* wife certainly wouldn't be *prodigal*.

She'd be too *judicious*, another word with a meaning similar to *prudent*. It, too, means "wise" and "having sound judgment." You probably never realized there were so many words that can use "wise" as a synonym. They are used interchangeably, but there are nuances that provide precise meanings.

Judicious, of course, is related to the word we use for the system of courts, our *judicial* system.

It includes examining, judging, and pronouncing a critical opinion—similar to the process used in court.

> A *judicious* decision is one that is the result of careful examination and consideration. It is more weighty than just being *prudent* and considering the consequences, and it includes more than native wisdom or even keen insight. It stresses the ability to reach wise decisions after analysis and study—no off-the-top-of-the-head pronouncements.

Omniscient is a useful word to add to our vocabularies. It denotes having total knowledge—but not necessarily mind-reading. *Omniscience* means "possessing understanding and insight." We use it to mean "aware of an impressive number of things or aspects of situations." We couldn't use it often to mean "complete knowledge of all things."

> *Omni* is a prefix meaning "all," and *scient* has the same root as "science"—to "know."

That's a good one for wrapping up descriptive words dealing with wisdom.

First we described physical characteristics of people:

> *Corpulent* and *obese:* Bulky, and fat, respectively.
>
> *Flaccid:* Flabby.

Maimed: Disabled, as with the loss of the use of a limb.

Bovine: Slow, sluggish, cowlike.

Pulchritude and *virile:* Beauty, and manly and vigorous, respectively.

Then we ran headlong into trouble with all that wisdom! See if you can separate *sagacious, acumen, prudent, judicious,* and *omniscient.* Notice that four are adjectives, but *acumen* is a noun.

Sagacious: Wise, discerning, of keen and far-sighted judgment.

Acumen: Keen insight and intuition.

Prudent: Wisely cautious because you think of the consequences.

Judicious: Having sound judgment and the ability to make a judgmental decision.

Omniscient: Having infinite awareness, understanding, and knowledge.

Now please complete Exercises 7 and 8 and Pretest 5. When you finish, we'll discuss relationships.

EXERCISE 7

Directions: On the lines in the following paragraph, write the words in parentheses that *best fit the meanings* of the sentences.

There seems to be a great deal of interest these days in weight reduction and exercise. No longer is it advisable to have a (1) _____ (*sagacious, corpulent*) frame. If one is (2) _____ (*obese, judicious*), he is looked upon almost with scorn. The friendly, (3) _____ (*flaccid, maimed*) Santa Claus figure is a thing of the past. In women, the stress is on (4) _____ (*pulchritude, acumen*) at all costs. For men, there must be (5) _____ (*omniscience, virility*) in all their actions. The problem with this current trend is that many have ignored (6) _____ (*prudence, virility*) and are committing every spare moment to exercise, jogging in the morning and visiting the spa at night. It would be (7) _____ (*judicious, restive*) if they curtailed some of this activity. In fact, several joggers have become (8) _____ (*querulous, maimed*) from bone fractures after running too much. (9) _____ (A *flaccid*, An *omniscient*) leader might remind his countrymen of the (10) _____ (*sagacious, irascible*) thoughts of Marcus Aurelius. Even the most (11) _____ (*bovine, malevolent*) and slow of thought can appreciate the (12) _____ (*acumen, virility*) of his famous saying, "Moderation in all things."

EXERCISE 8

Directions: On the lines in the following sentences, write the words in parentheses that *best fit the meanings* of the sentences.

1. To advance in a major health-promoting corporation, one should not be _____ (*corpulent, virile*).
2. A bear has to be _____ (*judicious, obese*) because he often goes without eating for three months.
3. Most women attempt to firm up their _____ (*omniscient, flaccid*) muscles before swimsuit season.
4. Although the one-legged wrestler was considered _____ (*bovine, maimed*) by many, he used his handicap to challenge himself in facing competitive situations.
5. A place where one enjoys _____ (*bovine, malevolent*) company is on the dairy farm.
6. _____ (*Pulchritude, Recalcitrance*) is one attribute that never goes out of favor.
7. The _____ (*obesity, virility*) of the Olympic performers was observed by all.
8. Confucius was one of the most _____ (*flaccid, sagacious*) men who ever lived.
9. Einstein possessed the _____ (*irascibility, acumen*) to unravel the secrets of the universe.
10. The boy showed no _____ (*depravity, prudence*) in driving the family car, and he often took chances that endangered the lives of others.
11. A most important task for the drama director is the _____ (*dour, judicious*) selection of the cast.
12. New owners claim that their computers are very nearly _____ (*prudent, omniscient*).

Pretest 5

Directions: Match the words in column A with the meanings in column B. On the line, write the word from column B that is *closest in meaning*.

A	B
1. proximity _____	temporary, hesitant
2. estrangement _____	actively negative feeling, aggression
3. affinity _____	show off
4. enmity _____	dislike of, aversion to, avoidance
5. antipathy _____	scoff at
6. hostility _____	hatred—often mutual
7. tentative _____	food specialist
8. flaunt _____	emotional separation
9. flout _____	attraction, similarity
10. gourmet _____	one who enjoys eating
11. gourmand _____	nearness

Section V, List 5

Before we begin analyzing relationships, let's return to the type of review we were doing in Section IV.

Using the words listed for each section, we found ten words that told what words *did*. Let's find some that tell what words *are*.

Words can be *acerbic* or *acrimonious*. Then there are *apocryphal* and *banal* words. They may be *colloquial* and still be *creditable*.

We hope they aren't *discursive* even when they're *extemporaneous*. And instead of being *extraneous,* we aim for words that are *germaine*.

Of course, they may also be *antonymns, homonyms,* or *synonyms*.

That's enough to show the process and whet the appetite if any still sounded unfamiliar.

What can words express? Words express *accolades* or *censure, cacophony* and *dissonance*. They are sometimes used as *codicils* or serve as *compendiums,* pinpoint *malapropisms* or play a role in *parodies*.

And, if you know the exact meanings of the twenty words we just used, our work has not been in vain.

If you don't remember one, cannot give a good synonym, go back to refresh your memory.

Now let's look at those relationships. We had *propinquity,* meaning "closeness" or even "kinship." Another word that means much the same thing is *proximity*.

> *Proximity* is often used to mean "immediately before or after" in a chain of events rather than physically near, but it can mean "physical closeness," too.
>
> The dictionary meaning for *proximity* is the "state of being near or next," and a synonym is "closeness."
>
> The most common misuse is in saying "close proximity." The two words mean the same thing, so one is extraneous.
>
> An antonym is *estrangement*.

The opposite of being close must be far, so that must mean to add distance, remove any *propinquity* or *proximity*.

To *estrange* means to "remove from a customary association" or to "arouse mutual *enmity*," especially where there has been affection or friendliness. It's often used in describing deteriorating relationships between husband and wife, partners, or co-workers who have had friendly harmony.

> *Estrangement* usually implies a separation—either physical or emotional.

That probably means that two people no longer have an *affinity* for each other. Now *affinity* is an unusual word. The root means "bordering on or related by marriage." With that somewhat divided meaning as a base, we use it in several differing contexts. The meaning changes with the use of different prepositions.

> When you speak of *affinity with* or *between*, the meaning is "likeness of temperament," "sympathy." The young prince enjoyed a special *affinity with* the young soldiers.

> There's *affinity to*, as in Caribbean music having a basic *affinity to* African music. Then it means "similarity" or "resemblance."

> When we use it with *for*—writers and actors having an *affinity for* each other—it means a "sympathetic attraction." It can also mean a "natural ability," as in, "He showed a great *affinity for* competitive sports."

All these uses and meanings are correct. *Affinity* changes from meaning "alike" to "sympathy" to "similarity" to "natural ability."

A less pleasant noun is *enmity*. It means "active hatred"

and "ill will," and the implication is that the feeling is mutual. One synonym is *antipathy*, but that suggests a desire to avoid or reject the object of the hatred.

When you read in the paper of the long-standing *enmity* between two families that resulted in an old-fashioned Chicago-style gang war, the *enmity* had reached the point of open *hostility*. It was too late for even *tentative* negotiations.

> *Tentative* is often the implied meaning of "negotiations"—a temporary peace for *negotiating*, for trying to talk over differences before relationships get worse.

As a matter of fact, many of our relationships are tentative. When we meet strangers, we even offer *tentative* smiles until we see what reaction we'll receive. If we are rewarded with a blank face or a frown, we withdraw the smile.

> We make *tentative* plans until we can test the reactions of others.

> Scientists publish *tentative* statements about their newest treatments until they can complete experiments that support what seems to be indicated. Then *tentative* means "hesitant" or "uncertain" or possibly "temporary."

There are two final pairs of words that cause confusion. The first two are *flaunt* and *flout*. They look alike, but their meanings aren't even close. Speculate what they mean if you don't know them.

You may have heard, "If you've got it, *flaunt* it!" From that you might assume *flaunt* means "show it"—or even "show it off"! The connotation is of being boastful or triumphant or even shameless.

> Old-fashioned discretion and modesty tend to make the *flaunting* of wealth, pulchritude, love affairs, or virility of questionable taste.

> But in that advice to *flaunt* it, you could be referring to sex appeal or commercial success, and in either, you might be criticized for *flaunting*.

> On the other hand, you can *flaunt* the flag or even a new mustache and merely be noticed as showing them.

> A *flaunt,* the noun, means a "display."

To *flaunt* the rules, meaning to "treat with contempt," is heard sometimes, but it is really considered a misuse of *flout* by people who get them confused.

> *Flout* does mean to "treat with contempt," to "openly show contempt" for something.

> We may *flout* convention when we choose to act in unacceptable ways, break family or company rules, or not follow the latest style. *Scoff* is a synonym.

> Used as a noun, *flout* means an "insult" or a "mockery."

The other pair is *gourmet* and *gourmand*. They both refer to good eating. One means a "person who is excessively fond of food and drink," and the other refers to the person who has made a study of and become an expert in fine food and drink. Which is which?

The *gourmet* is the specialist in the knowledge, and the *gourmand* is the specialist in eating.

Gourmet, retaining its French pronunciation, comes from a background meaning a "servant who was an assistant to the vintner, the winemaker, or the merchant." Sometimes he was also the wine taster, but he had no connection with food.

> We use it to mean both the person who has developed the ability to appreciate fine food and to describe the food itself. We have *gourmet* shops, *gourmet* restaurants, and *gourmet* recipes— all denoting (or at least implying) especially fine food appreciated only by the educated palate.

The *gourmand* buys in these shops, eats in these restaurants, and uses these recipes.

> The *gourmand* is heartily interested in good food and drink, probably with more emphasis on the eating than the preparing. There is the possible connotation of overdoing it.
>
> A *gourmet,* on the other hand, is still more of a taster than an overeater.

Now for one last review of our most recent words.

> *Proximity:* Nearness.
>
> *Estrangement:* Removal of former affection or friendliness.
>
> *Affinity:* Kinship, attraction, or likeness.

Enmity: Open hatred, often mutual.

Tentative: Not final, temporary or hesitant, conditional.

Flaunt and *flout:* To show off, and to show contempt for, respectively.

Gourmand: One who likes to eat.

Gourmet: Refers to an expert in fine food, or to food that is especially fine and appeals only to those with educated taste buds.

After you complete Exercises 9 and 10, we fade into the sunset like all good guides, leaving you with these thoughts: The words you use paint your portrait; be sure it's the one you want hung in your listeners' and readers' minds.

We should also reassure you that mastery of all the words we've discussed is *not* easy. If you aren't really on top of all of them, you probably have company. But the tools of attack—and reattack—are now yours forever.

You know how to use what the dictionaries tell you, you know how to speculate meanings from the use in context, and you have each word used in several different contexts. Future growth will come with your use of these and other new words.

Continue to expand your awareness of good vocabularies by reading extensively, especially the writings of challenging authors.

Enjoy words! And enjoy the knowledge that your readers and listeners are receiving exactly the thought you had in mind—and admiring your ability to present it.

EXERCISE 9

Directions: On the lines in the following paragraph, write the words in parentheses that *best fit the meanings* of the sentences.

The problem began simply enough. Jill was the (1) _____ (*sage*, *gourmet*) of the family, always preparing fancy dishes. Jim was the (2) _____ (*gourmand*, *ascetic*) who enjoyed nothing more than eating a special treat. At first, this love of food built an (3) _____ (*antipathy*, *affinity*) between the pair. But in time Jill began to (4) _____ (*flaunt*, *vacillate*) her skill at cooking. Then Jim began to (5) _____ (*delineate*, *flout*) every well-prepared meal. Soon (6) _____ (a *proximity*, an *antipathy*) developed in Jill for Jim. This led to a serious argument, climaxed by Jim's clearing the dishes by pulling the tablecloth off in one swift motion. This act of (7) _____ (*hostility*, *benevolence*) ended in an (8) _____ (*affinity*, *estrangement*) that could not be reconciled. Sadly, what had brought them together, a mutual love of food, led to their (9) _____ (*enmity*, *depravity*) for each other. In time neither could stand the (10) _____ (*sagaciousness*, *proximity*) of the other for any period of time. Eventually, Jim began making (11) _____ (*laconic*, *tentative*) suggestions for eating out, and they sought fast-food restaurants. The days of shared delicacies at home were over.

EXERCISE 10

Directions: On the lines in the following sentences, write the words in parentheses that *best fit the meanings* of the sentences.

1. After a period of _____ (*estrangement, status*), the couple separated.
2. The police said that the criminal was in the _____ (*brief, proximity*) of city hall.
3. He had _____ (an *affinity*, a *contingency*) for fine wine and fast cars.
4. The coach aroused the _____ (*criterion, enmity*) of the fans when he hit one of his own players.
5. Gandhi had _____ (a *codicil*, an *antipathy*) for violence and preached a doctrine of passive resistance.
6. The _____ (*circumspection, hostility*) between Syria and Israel has been one of the major problems of Middle Eastern politics.
7. The freshman quarterback was not _____ (*tentative, irascible*) when calling the plays; he knew what was needed.
8. Often the more competent the performer, the less likely he is to _____ (*vacillate, flaunt*) his talent.
9. If you _____ (*flout, mitigate*) listening to ideas of your fellow workers, you may end up missing some very good suggestions.
10. The _____ (*sage, gourmet*) is no longer found only in fine restaurants, but many households now boast of one in their own kitchens.
11. It is fine to be a _____ (*protagonist, gourmand*) provided you do not become obese in the practice.

Pretest 1

1. overwhelmed by emotion
2. extremely delighted
3. showy, colorful
4. lively, animated
5. pleasant, appropriate
6. balky, contrary
7. evil, corrupt
8. overly mournful
9. peevish, nagging
10. ill-natured, upsetting

Exercise 1

1. lugubrious
2. ecstatic
3. flamboyant
4. restive
5. querulous
6. enraptured
7. vivacious
8. felicitous
9. depraved
10. bilious

Exercise 2

1. ecstatic
2. flamboyant
3. vivacious
4. felicitous
5. depraved
6. restive
7. lugubrious
8. bilious
9. querulous
10. enraptured

Pretest 2

1. submissive, obedient
2. proper
3. pointlessly talkative
4. discursively talkative
5. wordy
6. fluent, possibly insincere
7. moralizing
8. inflexible, immovable
9. restrained, reluctant
10. concise, brief
11. inflated, padded
12. loud
13. waver, sway

Exercise 3

1. glib
2. bombastic
3. adamant
4. vacillate
5. vociferous
6. reticent
7. verbose
8. decorous
9. sententious
10. obsequious
11. laconic
12. loquacious
13. garrulously

Exercise 4

1. obsequious
2. decorous
3. garrulous
4. loquacious
5. glib
6. sententious
7. adamant
8. reticent
9. laconic
10. bombastic
11. vociferous
12. vacillating
13. verbose

Pretest 3

1. stern, sullen
2. worldly, bored
3. offensive, deserving hatred
4. practical
5. obstinate, defiant
6. irritable, easily angered
7. being or doing evil
8. doing good
9. cynic
10. enjoying people

Exercise 5

1. a dour
2. blasé
3. odious
4. benevolent
5. gregarious
6. misanthrope
7. recalcitrant
8. irascible
9. malevolent
10. pragmatic

Exercise 6

1. dour
2. blasé
3. odious
4. pragmatic
5. recalcitrant
6. irascible
7. malevolent
8. benevolent
9. gregarious
10. misanthrope

Pretest 4

1. bulky
2. fat
3. flabby, weakened
4. disabled
5. slow, sluggish, cowlike
6. beauty
7. vigor, energy
8. wise
9. keen insight
10. wise caution
11. judging wisely
12. all-knowing

Exercise 7

1. corpulent
2. obese
3. flaccid
4. pulchritude
5. virility
6. prudence
7. judicious
8. maimed
9. an omniscient
10. sagacious
11. bovine
12. acumen

Exercise 8

1. corpulent
2. obese
3. flaccid
4. maimed
5. bovine
6. pulchritude
7. virility
8. sagacious
9. acumen
10. prudence
11. judicious
12. omniscient

Pretest 5

1. nearness
2. emotional separation
3. attraction, similarity
4. hatred—often mutual
5. dislike of, aversion to, avoidance
6. actively negative feeling, aggression
7. temporary, hesitant
8. show off
9. scoff at
10. food specialist
11. one who enjoys eating

Exercise 9

1. gourmet
2. gourmand
3. affinity
4. flaunt
5. flout
6. an antipathy
7. hostility
8. estrangement
9. enmity
10. proximity
11. tentative

Exercise 10

1. estrangement
2. proximity
3. an affinity
4. enmity
5. an antipathy
6. hostility
7. tentative
8. flaunt
9. flout
10. gourmet
11. gourmand

Index to Words in Pretests

Section I — List 1 — Pronunciation

1. elucidate .... e-lu'ci-date
2. nuance.. nu'ance
3. critique .... cri-tique'
4. mnemonics.. mne-mon'ics
5. synonym .... syn'o-nym
6. denote .... de-note'
7. connotation .... con-no-ta'tion
8. imply .... im-ply'
9. infer .... in-fer'

Section I — List 2 — Pronunciation

1. cognizance .... cog'ni-zance
2. germane .... ger-mane'
3. succinct.. suc-cinct'
4. extraneous .... ex-tra'ne-ous
5. cerebration .... cer-e-bra'tion
6. prefix .... pre'fix

Section I — List 1 — Meaning

1. elucidate .... clarify
2. nuance .... shade of meaning
3. critique .... review carefully
4. mnemonics .... memory aids
5. synonym .... word with same meaning
6. denote .... mean
7. connotation .... suggested meaning
8. imply .... hint, suggest
9. infer .... deduce from facts

Section I — List 2 — Meaning

1. cognizance .... understanding
2. germane .... pertinent, related
3. succinct .... concise
4. extraneous .... unnecessary
5. cerebration .... thinking
6. prefix .... beginning of a word

Section I — List 3 — Pronunciation

1. ab—
2. ad—
3. com— or con—
4. de—
5. ex—
6. in—
7. in— (another meaning)
8. pre—
9. pro—
10. re—

(Pronunciation
may vary with
root word.)

Section I — List 4 — Pronunciation

1. abdicate ....ab'di-cate
2. abhor..ab-hor'
3. addendum ....ad-den'dum
4. adjunct ....ad'junct
5. concomitant ....con-com'i-tant
6. condescending ....con-de-scen'ding
7. delineate ....de-lin'e-ate
8. derisive ....de-ri'sive
9. ridiculous ....ri-dic'u-lous
10. expiate ....ex'pi-ate
11. atone ....a-tone'
12. expletive ....ex'ple-tive

Section I — List 3 — Meaning

1. ab— ....from, away
2. ad— ....to, toward
3. com— or con— ....with, together, thoroughly
4. de— ....from, down, away
5. ex— ....out of, from, former
6. in— ....in, into, on
7. in— (another meaning) not
8. pre— ....before, earlier than
9. pro— ....in favor of, forward
10. re— ....again, back

Section I — List 4 — Meaning

1. abdicate ....withdraw from
2. abhor....................detest, hate
3. addendum ....addition
4. adjunct ....added to, attached
5. concomitant .....accompanying
6. condescending...patronizing
7. delineate ....draw, clarify
8. derisive ....scornful
9. ridiculous ....absurd, laughable
10. expiate ....make amends
11. atone ....reconcile
12. expletive ....meaningless expression, profanity

Section I — List 5 — Pronunciation

1. induce..in-duce'
2. inadvertently...............................in-ad-ver'tent-ly
3. precept ....pre'cept
4. prodigious..................................pro-di'gious
5. propinquity.................................pro-pin'qui-ty
6. resurgence.................................re-sur'gence
7. anomalous.................................a-nom'a-lous
8. apocryphal.................................a-poc'ry-phal
9. portentous.................................por-ten'tous

Section I — List 6 — Pronunciation

1. erudite ....er'u-dite
2. esoteric.....................................es-o-ter'ic
3. enigma ....e-nig'ma
4. cacophony ....ca-coph'o-ny
5. dissonance ....dis'so-nance
6. corroboration ....cor-rob-o-ra'tion
7. homogeneity...............................ho-mo-ge-ne'i-ty
8. acrimonious ....ac-ri-mo'ni-ous
9. bellicose ....bel'li-cose
10. nefarious ....ne-far'i-ous
11. accolade ....ac'co-lade
12. paragon ....par'a-gon
13. emulate......................................em'u-late

Section I — List 5 — Meaning

1. induce...................................lead to
2. inadvertently ....unintentionally
3. precept ....principle, example
4. prodigious ....enormous
5. propinquity ....nearness
6. resurgence............................renewal
7. anomalous............................irregular
8. apocryphal...........................of dubious validity
9. portentous............................ominous

Section I — List 6 — Meaning

1. erudite ....displaying knowledge, learned
2. esoteric ....hidden, secret
3. enigma ....puzzle
4. cacophony.................disharmony, harsh sound
5. dissonance ....noise, lack of agreement
6. corroboration ....confirmation, support
7. homogeneity.............similarity, uniformity
8. acrimonious ....bitter, harsh
9. bellicose....................argumentative, belligerent
10. nefarious ....flagrantly wicked
11. accolade....................praise
12. paragon ....perfect example, model
13. emulate ....imitate

Section II — List 1 — Pronunciation

1. serendipity...ser-en-dip'i-ty
2. pedigree...ped'i-gree
3. exigency...ex'i-gen-cy
4. emergency..e-mer'gen-cy
5. contingency...con-tin'gen-cy
6. crisis ....cri'sis
7. dire ....dire
8. strait ....strait
9. extricate..ex'tri-cate

Section II — List 2 — Pronunciation

1. anesthetic ....an-es-thet'ic
2. anesthesia ....an-es-the'sia
3. anesthetist...................................an-es'the-tist
4. anesthesiologist......................an-es-the-si-ol'o-gist
5. data ....da'ta
6. status ....stat'us
7. stratum ....stra'tum
8. candelabra....................................can-de-la'bra
9. agenda ....a-gen'da
10. criterion ....cri-ter'i-on
11. phenomenon..............................phe-nom'e-non

Section II — List 1 — Meaning

1. serendipity...aptitude for finding unexpected bonuses
2. pedigree ......ancestral line
3. exigency ......urgency
4. emergency...unexpected occurrence needing action
5. contingency..possibility
6. crisis..............turning point
7. dire ....desperate
8. strait..............tight place, narrow passage
9. extricate ......untangle, free

Section II — List 2 — Meaning

1. anesthetic ....gas or drug producing anesthesia
2. anesthesia..........loss of sensation, feeling
3. anesthetist ....one who administers anesthetic
4. anesthesiologist.doctor who specializes in anesthesia
5. data......................information, facts
6. status ....position, social standing
7. stratum ....a layer
8. candelabra ....a branched candlestick
9. agenda ....plan, schedule
10. criterion ....a standard for basing judgment
11. phenomenon ....an observable fact or event

Section II — List 3 — Pronunciation

1. circumference .... cir-cum'fer-ence
2. circumlocution .... cir-cum-lo-cu'tion
3. circumvent .... cir-cum-vent'
4. circumnavigate .... cir-cum-nav'i-gate
5. circumspect .... cir'cum-spect
6. contraindication .... con-tra-in-di-ca'tion
7. contradict .... con-tra-dict'
8. pseudoscience .... pseu-do-sci'ence
9. pseudopregnancy .... pseu-do-preg'nan-cy
10. pseudotuberculosis .... pseu-do-tu-ber-cu-lo'sis
11. subordinate .... sub-or'di-nate
12. subterranean .... sub-ter-ran'e-an

Section II — List 4 — Pronunciation

1. abstention .... ab-sten'tion
2. consummate (verb) .... con'sum-mate (verb)
3. consummate (adj) .... con-sum'mate (adj)
4. cosmopolitan .... cos-mo-pol'i-tan
5. cosmopolite .... cos-mop'o-lite
6. cosmos .... cos'mos
7. cosmography .... cos-mog'ra-phy
8. malapropism .... mal'a-prop-ism
9. ubiquitous .... u-biq'ui-tous
10. compendium .... com-pen'di-um
11. ludicrous .... lu'di-crous
12. obfuscate .... ob'fus-cate

Section II — List 3 — Meaning

1. circumference ....distance around a circle
2. circumlocution ....talking around the point
3. circumvent ....go around, avoid
4. circumnavigate ....sail around, bypass
5. circumspect ....prudent, wise
6. contraindication ....opposite or false indication
7. contradict ....speak in opposition, refute
8. pseudoscience ....false science
9. pseudopregnancy..........false pregnancy
10. pseudotuberculosis ......not real tuberculosis
11. subordinate ....inferior in rank
12. subterranean ....underground

Section II — List 4 — Meaning

1. abstention................act of voluntarily refraining from
2. consummate(verb).bring to completion (verb)
3. consummate(adj)...perfect, complete (adj)
4. cosmopolitan ....worldly, at home anywhere
5. cosmopolite ....rich and sophisticated person
6. cosmos ....universe
7. cosmography ....science of the order of nature
8. malapropism ....misuse of words
9. ubiquitous...............everywhere present
10. compendium ....summary, list
11. ludicrous ....laughable, ridiculous
12. obfuscate.................to confuse

Section II — List 5 — Pronunciation

1. progeny .... prog'e-ny
2. prodigy .... prod'i-gy
3. reprehend .... repre-hend'
4. comprehend .... com-pre-hend'
5. oracular .... o-rac'u-lar
6. vernacular .... ver-nac'u-lar
7. deranged .... de-ranged'
8. epitaph .... ep'i-taph
9. epithet .... ep'i-thet
10. censor .... cen'sor
11. censure .... cen'sure
12. censer .... cen'ser
13. sensor .... sen'sor
14. equable .... eq'ua-ble
15. equitable .... eq'ui-ta-ble
16. entomology .... en-to-mol'o-gy
17. etymology .... et-y-mol'o-gy

Section II — List 6 — Pronunciation

1. —logy
2. —ly   (Pronunciation
3. —ful   may vary with
4. —ship   root word.)
5. —like

Section II — List 5 — Meaning

1. progeny ....descendants
2. prodigy ....talented, bright child, omen
3. reprehend ....to criticize
4. comprehend ....understand
5. oracular ....authoritative
6. vernacular ....common language
7. deranged ....disturbed
8. epitaph ....inscription on tombstone
9. epithet..........................descriptive phrase, profanity
10. censor ....delete
11. censure ....criticize
12. censer ....incense burner
13. sensor ....responsive cell
14. equable........................uniform, steady
15. equitable ....fair, just
16. entomology ....study of insects
17. etymology.....................study of words

Section II — List 6 — Meaning

1. —logy..science or theory of
2. —ly ....like
3. —ful ....characteristic of
4. —ship ....characteristic of
5. —like ....characteristic of

Section III — List 1 — Pronunciation

1. literate ....lit′er-ate
2. illiterate ....il-lit′er-ate
3. legible ....leg′i-ble
4. readable ....read′a-ble
5. unreadable ....un-read′a-ble
6. unintelligible ....un-in-tel′li-gi-ble
7. homonyms ....hom′o-nyms
8. antonyms ....an′to-nyms
9. articulate ....ar-tic′u-late
10. antithesis.................................an-tith′-e-sis
11. abnegate ....ab′ne-gate
12. discursive ....dis-cur′sive
13. banal...ba-nal′

Section III — List 2 — Pronunciation

1. diffident ....dif′fi-dent
2. docile ....doc′ile
3. deprecate ....dep′re-cate
4. depreciate ....de-pre′ci-ate
5. disparage ....dis-par′age
6. sensual ....sen′su-al
7. sensuous ....sen′su-ous
8. continual ....con-tin′u-al
9. continuous...............................con-tin′u-ous
10. continuity ....con-ti-nu′l-ty
11. concurrent ....con-cur′rent
12. consecutive ....con-sec′u-tive

Section III — List 1 — Meaning

1. literate .... able to read/write, cultured
2. illiterate .... unable to read/write, uncultured
3. legible .... clear, easily read
4. readable .... easily read, interesting
5. unreadable .... cannot be read, uninteresting
6. unintelligible .... not understandable
7. homonyms .... words that sound alike
8. antonyms .... words with opposite meanings
9. articulate .... speak clearly, jointed
10. antithesis .... direct contrast, opposite position
11. abnegate .... deny, renounce
12. discursive .... rambling
13. banal .... commonplace, trite

Section III — List 2 — Meaning

1. diffident .... shy, reserved
2. docile .... easy to lead, tractable
3. deprecate .... disapprove
4. depreciate .... devalue, belittle
5. disparage .... degrade, discredit
6. sensual .... physically pleasing
7. sensuous .... aesthetically enjoyable
8. continual .... repeated regularly
9. continuous .... unceasing, uninterrupted
10. continuity .... continuing in sequence
11. concurrent .... at the same time
12. consecutive .... in sequence

Section III — List 3 — Pronunciation

1. uni
2. mono
3. bi
4. tri
5. quad (quadra, quadri)
6. multi
7. credible .... cre'di-ble
8. credulous .... cred'u-lous
9. creditable .... cred'it-a-ble
10. historic .... his-tor'ic
11. historical .... his-tor'i-cal
12. acerbic .... a-cer'bic
13. ascetic .... as-cet'ic
14. aesthetic .... aes-thet'ic
15. flammable .... flam'ma-ble
16. nonflammable .... non-flam'ma-ble
17. inflammatory .... in-flam'ma-to-ry

Section III — List 4 — Pronunciation

1. activate .... ac'ti-vate
2. activism .... ac'ti-vism
3. initiate .... in-it'i-ate
4. enterprise .... en'ter-prise
5. entrepreneur .... en-tre-pre-neur'
6. ascertain .... as-cer-tain'
7. minimize .... min'i-mize
8. maximize .... max'i-mize

Section III — List 3 — Meaning

1. uni— ....one
2. mono— ....one
3. bi— ....two
4. tri— ....three
5. quad—
   (quadra—, quadri—) four
6. multi— ....many
7. credible ....believable, plausible
8. credulous ....gullible, childlike
9. creditable ....worthy of praise or trust
10. historic ....significant in history
11. historical ....of or relating to history
12. acerbic ....bitingly severe, critical
13. ascetic ....practicing self-denial, hermit
14. aesthetic ....appreciating beauty
15. flammable ....highly combustible
16. nonflammable ....not combustible
17. inflammatory ....arousing emotion, exciting

Section III — List 4 — Meaning

1. activate ....set in motion, make active
2. activism ....action on controversial issue
3. initiate ....begin, start
4. enterprise ....undertaking of some scope
5. enterpreneur ....organizer/manager of business
6. ascertain ....make certain, determine
7. minimize ....lessen, reduce to smaller
8. maximize ....increase, make most of

Section III — List 5 — Pronunciation

1. regardless .... re-gard'less
2. importune .... im-por-tune'
3. opportune .... op-por-tune'
4. rectitude .... rec'ti-tude
5. righteous .... right'eous

Section IV — List 1 — Pronunciation

1. idiolect .... id'i-o-lect
2. dialect .... di'a-lect
3. colloquialism .... col-lo'qui-al-ism
4. jargon .... jar'gon
5. venue .... ven'ue
6. beneficiary .... ben-e-fi'ci-ar-y
7. brief .... brief
8. codicil .... cod'i-cil
9. catalyst .... cat'a-lyst
10. exacerbate .... ex-ac'er-bate
11. excoriate .... ex-cor'i-ate
12. stellar .... stel'lar
13. arboreal .... ar-bo're-al

Section III — List 5 — Meaning

1. regardless ....in spite of
2. importune ....urge persistently, beg urgently
3. opportune ....suitable, convenient
4. rectitude ....correct judgment
5. righteous ....morally correct

Section IV — List 1 — Meaning

1. idiolect ....individual speech pattern
2. dialect ....regional speech pattern
3. colloquialism ......conversational expression
4. jargon...................slang or specialized vocabulary
5. venue ....location
6. beneficiary ....gift recipient
7. brief ....legal document, concise, to coach
8. codicil..................addition to a will
9. catalyst................agent of change
10. exacerbate..........aggravate, make worse
11. excoriate ....denounce, remove skin
12. stellar ....outstanding, superior
13. arboreal ....treelike

Section IV — List 2 — Pronunciation

1. Interface ....in'ter-face
2. debug ....de-bug'
3. input ....in'put
4. throughput..................................through'put
5. output ....out'put
6. silicon ....sil'i-con
7. silicone ....sil'i-cone
8. ad lib..ad-lib'
9. improvise ....im'pro-vise
10. extemporaneous ....ex-tem-po-ra'ne-ous
11. scenario ....sce-nar'i-o
12. protagonist ....pro-tag'on-ist
13. parody..par'o-dy

Section IV — List 3 — Pronunciation

1. parsimonious ....par-si-mo'ni-ous
2. niggardly ....nig'gard-ly
3. prodigal ....prod'i-gal
4. altruistic......................................al-tru-is'tic
5. taciturn ....tac'i-turn
6. loquacious ....lo-qua'cious
7. apathetic ....ap-a-thet'ic
8. lethargic.....................................le-thar'gic
9. militate..mil'i-tate
10. mitigate ....mit'i-gate
11. ingenious.....................................in-gen'ious
12. ingenuous ....in-gen'u-ous
13. specious ....spe'cious
14. plausible ....plau'si-ble

Section IV — List 2 — Meaning

1. interface ....work together, communicate
2. debug............................remove errors
3. input............................opinion, comment
4. throughput ....productivity
5. output ....something produced, result
6. silicon ....nonmetallic element used in electronics
7. silicone ....organic compound used for lubricants
8. ad lib ....as desired, freely
9. improvise ....make up on spot
10. extemporaneous...........without notes
11. scenario......................plot outline
12. protagonist.................leading character
13. parody ....imitation of style

Section IV — List 3 — Meaning

1. parsimonious ....stingy
2. niggardly ....miserly, tightfisted
3. prodigal ....extravagant, profuse
4. altruistic......................devoted to others
5. taciturn........................silent, uncommunicative
6. loquacious....................talkative
7. apathetic ....showing no emotion
8. lethargic.......................drowsy, sluggish
9. militate ....work against
10. mitigate ....reduce severity
11. ingenious ....clever, inventive
12. ingenuous ....unsophisticated, innocent
13. specious.......................false look of, invalidity
14. plausible ....apparently valid

Section IV — List 4 — Pronunciation

1. chic .... chic
2. clique .... clique
3. croissant .... crois-sant'
4. caramel .... car'a-mel
5. abdomen .... ab'do-men
6. adult .... a-dult'
7. apricot .... a'pri-cot
8. arctic .... arc'tic
9. superfluous .... su-per'flu-ous

Section IV — List 5 — Pronunciation

1. anti
2. ante
3. inter
4. intra
5. retro
6. less
7. ness, hood, dom
8. ish
9. ward

(Pronunciation
may vary with
root word.)

Section IV — List 4 — Meaning

1. chic .... stylish, elegant
2. clique .... exclusive group
3. croissant .... crescent-shaped roll
4. caramel .... cooked sugar sauce, confection
5. abdomen .... midsection of body, stomach area
6. adult .... mature, full grown
7. apricot .... small fruit related to plum
8. arctic .... characteristic of North Pole, frigid
9. superfluous .... extra, unnecessary

Section IV — List 5 — Meaning

1. anti— .... against, opposed to
2. ante— .... before, earlier
3. inter— .... between
4. intra— .... within
5. retro— .... backward
6. —less .... without, lacking
7. —ness, —hood, —dom state, quality, condition of
8. —ish .... relating to, characteristic of
9. —ward .... direction of

Section V — List 1 — Pronunciation

1. ecstatic ....ec-stat'ic
2. enraptured..en-rap'tured
3. flamboyant ....flam-boy'ant
4. vivacious ....vi-va'cious
5. felicitous..fe-lic'i-tous
6. restive ....res'tive
7. depraved ....de-praved'
8. lugubrious..lu-gu'bri-ous
9. querulous...quer'u-lous
10. bilious ....bil'ious

Section V — List 2 — Pronunciation

1. obsequious ....ob-se'qui-ous
2. decorous ....dec'o-rous
3. garrulous ....gar'ru-lous
4. loquacious..lo-qua'cious
5. verbose...ver-bose'
6. glib..glib
7. sententious ....sen-ten'tious
8. adamant ....ad'a-mant
9. reticent ....ret'i-cent
10. laconic..la-con'ic
11. bombastic ....bom-bas'tic
12. vociferous ....vo-cif'er-ous
13. vacillate..va'cil-late

Section V — List 1 — Meaning

1. ecstatic .... overwhelmed by emotion
2. enraptured .... extremely delighted
3. flamboyant .... showy, colorful
4. vivacious .... lively, animated
5. felicitous .... pleasant, appropriate
6. restive .... balky, contrary
7. depraved .... evil, corrupt
8. lugubrious .... overly mournful
9. querulous .... peevish, nagging
10. bilious .... ill-natured, upsetting

Section V — List 2 — Meaning

1. obsequious .... submissive, obedient
2. decorous .... proper
3. garrulous .... pointlessly talkative
4. loquacious .... discursively talkative
5. verbose .... wordy
6. glib .... fluent, possibly insincere
7. sententious .... moralizing
8. adamant .... inflexible, immovable
9. reticent .... restrained, reluctant
10. laconic .... concise, brief
11. bombastic .... inflated, padded
12. vociferous .... loud
13. vacillate .... waver, sway

Section V — List 3 — Pronunciation

1. dour...dour
2. blasé ....bla-se'
3. odious...o'di-ous
4. pragmatic...prag-mat'ic
5. recalcitrant..re-cal'ci-trant
6. irascible ....i-ras'ci-ble
7. malevolent...ma-lev'o-lent
8. benevolent...be-nev'o-lent
9. misanthrope ....mis'an-thrope
10. gregarious ....gre-gar'i-ous

Section V — List 4 — Pronunciation

1. corpulent...cor'pu-lent
2. obese ....o-bese'
3. flaccid..flac'cid
4. maimed ....maimed
5. bovine ....bo'vine
6. pulchritude..pul'chri-tude
7. virility ....vi-ril'i-ty
8. sagacious ....sa-ga'cious
9. acumen ....a-cu'men
10. prudence ....pru'dence
11. judicious ....ju-di'cious
12. omniscient ....om-nis'cient

Section V — List 3 — Meaning

1. dour .... stern, sullen
2. blasé .... worldly, bored
3. odious .... offensive, deserving hatred
4. pragmatic .... practical
5. recalcitrant .... obstinate, defiant
6. irascible .... irritable, easily angered
7. malevolent .... being or doing evil
8. benevolent .... doing good
9. misanthrope .... cynic
10. gregarious .... enjoying people

Section V — List 4 — Meaning

1. corpulent .... bulky
2. obese .... fat
3. flaccid .... flabby, weakened
4. maimed .... disabled
5. bovine .... slow, sluggish, cowlike
6. pulchritude .... beauty
7. virility .... vigor, energy
8. sagacious .... wise
9. acumen .... keen insight
10. prudence .... wise caution
11. judicious .... judging wisely
12. omniscient .... all-knowing

Section V — List 5 — Pronunciation

1. proximity......................................prox-im'i-ty
2. estrangement...............................es-trange'ment
3. affinity..af-fin'i-ty
4. enmity...en'mi-ty
5. antipathy.....................................an-tip'a-thy
6. hostility......................................hos-til'-i-ty
7. tentative.....................................ten'ta-tive
8. flaunt..flaunt
9. flout..flout
10. gourmet......................................gour-met'
11. gourmand....................................gour-mand'

Section V — List 5 — Meaning

1. proximity .... nearness
2. estrangement ... emotional separation
3. affinity .... attraction, similarity
4. enmity .... hatred—often mutual
5. antipathy .... dislike of, aversion to, avoidance
6. hostility .... actively negative feeling, aggression
7. tentative .... temporary, hesitant
8. flaunt ...., show off
9. flout .... scoff at
10. gourmet .... food specialist
11. gourmand .... one who enjoys eating